DIRECTIONS TO HARMONHY

How to Use Feng Shui in Your Daily Life

An Illustrated Guide to
Tranquility and Good Fortune

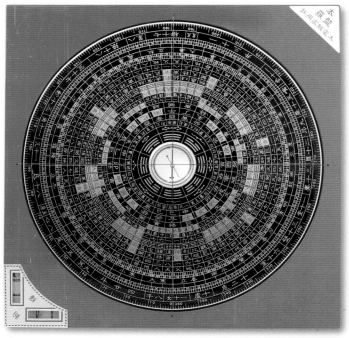

Feng Shui Compass (p.15)

Feng Shui Compass (p.16)

Feng Shui Compass with a carry bag (p.16)

Transparent Feng Shui Compass (p.17)

Feng Shui Compass
Wall Hanging (p.17)

Feng Shui Measurement Ruler
(p.21-22)

Feng Shui Energy Stabilizer (p.18)

Ba Gua
Mirror
(p.26-27)

Feng Shui tile to
Improve Twelve
Directions (p.22-24)

Dragon Holding up a Ball (p.49)

Laughing Dragon (p.45)

Ascending Dragon with Seven Positioned Crystal Balls (p.43)

Ornament Illuminating the Energy of Heavens and Earth (p.51-52)

Feng Shui Sansuiryu (p.41)

Good Fortune Goblet (p.35-36)

Five Fingered Wishing Dragon (p.42)

Dragon Holding a Crystal Ball (p.52-53)

Pixiu (p.70-72)

White Tiger (p.56)

Black Tortoise (p.59)

Vermilion Bird (p.60-62)

Azure Dragon (p.55)

Lion (p.62-63)

Copper Ba Gua Lion Tile (p.65)

Horse (p.66-67)

Feng Shui Money Panther Ornament (p.77)

Pixiu (p.70)

Chinese Unicorns (p.69)

Yaazu (p.75-76)

Portable Yaazu (p.76)

Chinese Phoenix Disk (p.80)

Arowana (p.77-78)

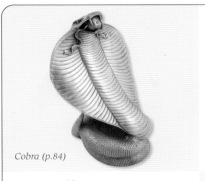
Cobra (p.84)

Turtle (p.83)

Chicken (p.85)

Three Legged Toad (p.86-87)

Long Gui (p.73-74)

Amethyst Dome (p.90)

Crystal Healing Lamp (p.97-98)

Treasure Agate (p.91)

A Crystal Ball Inserted in a Purple Bag (p.94)

Healing-Cut-Crystal (p.99-100)

Amethyst Pebbles (p.95-96)

Rose Quartz Pebbles (p.96)

Gold Rutilated Quartz Pebbles (p.97)

Crystal Pebbles (p.95)

Feng Shui Fountains

Dragon King (p.161)

Platform Type Basin (p.163)

Affectionate Type Basin (p.162-163)

Good Luck God with Potbelly (p.162)

Seven Star Sword made of Copper (p.111)

Universal Light Fixing Hanging (p.124-125)

Feng Shui Made of Old Coins (p.136)

Copper Idol of Guan Yu (p.150-151)

Stone Monument (p.114)

A Latticed Ball (p.112)

Dragon Pendant (p.125)

Gold Ingot (p.140)

Old Coins (p.141)

Fortune God (p.130)

Lion and Ba Gua Mirror (p.113)

Gourd (p.108)

Ba Gua Incense Burner (p.117)

Evil Removing Incense (p.119)

Gold Rutilated Quartz (p.158)

Green Phantom
(p.158)

Gold Rutilated Quartz(p.158)

Various Power Stone Seal (p.158)

FGVermilion Ink-pad with Dragon
(p.159)

風
FENG SHUI
水

中国正統

Contents

Prologue

Chapter 1

Chapter 2

Use the dragon's power to its maximum!

CHAPTER 3

Get hold of powerful fortune with the power of animals

CHAPTER 4

Attain your desire with the power of crystal and stones

CHAPTER 5

Dispose negative energy and stabilize energy ...104

CHAPTER 6

Luck will change just by carrying or affixing these items! 120

CHAPTER 7

More good fortune comes when combined with other items

CHAPTER 8

Improve your fortune using color, sound, light and fragrance!

CHAPTER 9

Recommended items to meet your desire and objectives

PROLOGUE

Feng Shui begins
with arranging
the surroundings
around you

Feng Shui is the study of maintaining the environment.

Most people probably know about or heard about the word "feng shui". And, since many people have begun to adopt feng shui in their lives, many feng shui items are now available. You can even get them from mail order. But many imitations of genuine feng shui items are also being sold and one must be careful about purchases.

Feng shui, which seems suddenly to have become popular in Japan, has in fact, has been a core thought in the East for more than 4,000 years. The bases of Kigaku (fortune telling based on Chinese twelve year cycle) and Houigaku (fortune telling based on directions) in Japan have their origins there.

There are many of those who know little about feng shui and might think it is a kind of fortune telling, a charm, or a superstition without scientific foundation. However, this is not so. Feng shui is, in a word, is a study of environmental maintenance that determines the good and bad of topography with directions or length, purifies the living and business environment, and call in the fortune of wealth and such. People have been utilizing for centuries the study of environmental maintenance in order to make life comfortable and affluent in China. It has influenced not only buildings but also on politics and town planning. Why are people in the East so fixated on feng shui? Obviously it is to increase one's fortune, but there are five thoughts in Chinese culture to explain this interest: destiny, fate, feng shui, service, and learning. These words came about when an old man looked back on his life and a made a list of words important to his life.

Based upon these words, the most influential factor in life is destiny, the second influential factor in life is fate, and feng shui is listed as the third influential factor. The forth factor is a service which is to help out others by doing volunteer service. Learning, the most important factor now in Japan, is ranked fifth.

You are born with your destiny, and it cannot be changed no matter what you do. If you want to improve your life, you might think of studying and offering services. However, rather than doing that, you should arrange your feng shui environment first. Then you will offer services and pursue learning. That is a faster way to improve your fortune. In other words, no matter how much effort you put in, you will not get good results unless your feng shui environment is arranged.

Then how do we arrange feng shui? Primarily, feng shui is composed of the five Eastern thoughts. They are life, telling fortune, aspect, medicine, and a mountain. Feng shui belongs to the aspect, and it determines how a person's form influences positively or negatively from palms, physiognomy and so on. However, feng shui mainly judges how topography influences people.

The most important thing in feng shui is the flow of energy called "ki". You might think it is not easy to understand this concept, but it means energy exists in everything. The energy flowing on the earth is thought to have great influence in changing one's fortune. In feng shui, the road for energy is to flow as "a dragon vein" and the place for energy to gather as "a dragon hole." It is said that good energy that brings good luck flows along the dragon vein and gathers in the dragon hole.

The area that good energy congregates is called an ideal topography for the four Taoist gods. There are a Black Tortoise in the north, an Azure Dragon in the east, a Vermilion Bird in the south, and a White Tiger in the west. As far as energy in feng shui is concerned, this is the best geographical location, and it is treasured. It is said when a house or business is built in such a location, the house will flourish, and the business will prosper.

Nevertheless, it is very difficult to acquire such property. As the land development has progressed, these ideal lands became scarce. Even if one is found, it is very rare that the property will be sold as it is a very comfortable place for the owner to live. However, you do not need to give up the idea of looking for an ideal place because there is always a flow of energy on the earth. There are methods to increase your fortune to have a clear picture of energy flow by learning the directional use and utilizing feng shui items, and collect good energy and good luck.

The study of Feng Shui based upon the fundamentals of "Changing Law", cosmic dual forces (yin and yang) and the five elements (metal, wood, water, fire and earth) in Chinese cosmology

I would like to explain a little bit about the ideology of Changing Law upon which feng shui is based. Changing Law was formulated about 2,800 years ago in the dynasty of Western Zhou. It is an important book as Eastern philosophy was based upon this school of thought. The basis of Changing Law is about cosmic dual forces (yin and yang) and five elements (metal, wood, water, fire, and earth) in Chinese cosmology. It is clear even from the name Changing Law that things do change. The Chinese characters of Changing Law are 易経、and the first character 易 has combined radicals of the sun and the moon. Even from this, it is evident that Changing Law is about the changes caused by associating yin and yang. Because all worldly things are transitory, anything with forms will perish; and yet, new things will be formed. Whether you like it or not, all things in nature are going to change.

However, do you know that there is one thing that never changes? The answer is that everything is going to change, and this fact itself is never going to change. The eternal change caused by yin and yang is a certain rule. The Chinese cultural sphere including Japan have believed the law that the end, or death, of temporal things results in rebirth, in a cycle of ends and beginning. This theory is based upon the Chinese classic, Zishi Tongjian: Comprehensive Mirror for Aid in Government, and Eastern people believe that everything is ruled by this law.

That is to say that the environment surrounding the earth and the minds of people are changing. On the other hand, we usually look for security and do not accept changes easily. I myself believe that many problems and worries that people encounter are caused by the fact that the desire to have security cannot catch up with changing circumstances. when a person meets a person of the opposite sex, a friendship starts at first; as the friendship becomes more intense, his or her mind and the environment surrounding them are going to change. At first, he or she accepts this change excitedly. However, as the friendship changes to a love affair, they tend to look for security and become afraid of changes caused by the partner's behavior. If one of them changes his or her mind and leaves the partner, he or she will be hurt. Sometimes, he or she cannot accept the change of heart and might even develop into someone like a stalker. If he or she understood the teaching of Changing Law, he or she will accept the change of heart as a natural phenomenon, or before the change of heart occurs, he or she will change how to deal with the partner or change the circumstance and cope with the situation so that the break up will not happen.

Changes are caused by the rules of yin and yang. They indicate the opposite extreme, and it symbolizes the power of giving birth to things. The heaven and the earth, light and shadow, the sun and the moon, a man and a woman are all pairs and show the relationship of yin and yang. Everything in the world is consisted of yin and yang, and it is keeping its balance while constantly changing. Feng shui is also based upon the fundamentals of "Changing Law", cosmic dual forces (yin and yang) and the five elements (metal, wood, water, fire and earth) in Chinese cosmology. The important key word, ki (energy) is born from the same rule, and "ki" is always changing.

Are you feeling the earth's energy?

We observed astronomy and had a clear picture of topographic changes from ancient times. By doing so, we felt the energy of the universe and tried to use it. Animals start running before an earthquake occurs or birds and insects disappear before it begins to rain. They do this because they sense the change of energy. Essentially, humans also have the ability to feel the change of energy. For instance, if you had taken a therapeutic walk in the forest, you must have noticed that the aroma of trees made you relaxed and healed your mind. What had affected your mind and body was the existence of energy. The reason you relaxed was due to the energy coming from the forest transmitted to your body through the five senses.

Have you ever felt that you don't feel comfortable at home, an office or a hotel? This also relates to the influence caused by energy. However, humans are adaptable, so we soon get used to the environment and forget the initial uncomfortable feeling. Nevertheless, energy influences our emotional conditions greatly. When energy is bad, you get depressed, and when energy is good, you feel happier. Everything is based on the balance of yin and yang. If there is more negative energy where you are, your life energy (positive energy) will be absorbed there in order to keep a balance of yin and yang. On the other hand, more positive energy is found at where you live, it always takes in positive energy and makes your life energy stronger. This is what it means to maintain the feng shui environment.

Energy comes out from all things including humans, sphere, the ground, water, fire, metals, animals and plants. There is both energy that we can feel and cannot feel, and we live influenced by both energy. We actually live feeling energy surrounding us, but we do not pay much attention to it.

In order to determine the influence by energy, a certain method is used in feng shui. The methods called "form and landscape" are used to determine the visual influence and the non-visual influence respectively. Feeling the flow of energy, it will improve the balance of energy.

I hear a lot of griping from people: "My business is not doing well", "I am bothered by my relationship with others", and "only the bad things continue to happen." In order to get out of these situations, they make all possible efforts, and they say that it is like rowing a boat as hard as they can against the wind. It is of course important to do your best; however, should it not be better to have an unfavorable wind changed to a favorable wind at first? Likewise, if you are putting all

your efforts so that your dream comes true, you will get there sooner if a favorable wind pushes you. This is what the improvement of feng shui is all about.

Most people tend to solve the problems using the same way: try my best at any cost, get angry at people indiscriminately, tolerate quietly, etc. If your problems do not go away, you would repeat the same methods and reach the limits. When you change by improving feng shui, the flow of energy will change. To simply put it, make sure to stop the intrusion of negative energy and heighten the activity of good energy. Plan a device to give the power of creation and make it last permanently. As energy in a place changes, your mood will change as well. Consequently, you would look at a situation from different angles, or you might even be able to look at it objectively. As you will cope with your problems differently, the result will change as well. Then your relationship with others and your fortune will move smoothly.

If you think clearly and simply and act accordingly, power will follow you. There is an essential point for improving your feng shui environment. The essential point is that you will start to change the environment one or two steps above your current environment. Without a doubt, energy there will change. Believe in what you have decided to do, and you will move on.

The people who live in the modern era, especially those who believed in Americanized rationalism after the World

War II, tend not to believe in the energy that cannot be physically seen. Whether you can see it or not, would not it be
better if the places with which you are connected—a house,
a store or an office—became comfortable? If you don't believe in it, think of it as an incarnation. Think of it as if your
pushing will be further helped by an unforeseen power's
pushing, and how would you like to actually feel that the
pushing is arranging and maintaining feng shui.

As I said in the beginning, feng shui is a study of environmental maintenance that calls in good luck and improves
your fate. As you will utilize feng shui, you will be able to
live and work in comfortable space, increase your potential
and heighten your later fortune.

A method to improve your fortune
you can do now – "Kasatu Fuusui"
(Eliminating negative energy)

After becoming familiar with the meaning of feng shui, it
is natural that everyone wants to live in an ideal topography for the four Taoist gods or in the house which is surrounded by good feng shui.

However, excluding the place where all the positive feng
shui elements are found, in the Palace Museum in Forbidden
City in China, we rarely find a house or a building with a perfect feng shui arrangement.
You always find something wrong in the
house or in the building, but it is not
realistic to move out or reconstruct
the house or the building as it is very

costly.

If you are thinking of moving into a new house, an office or a store and if you are going to build a building, you can construct it according to feng shui. However, nowadays, we tend to move into a ready built apartment or a condo. Even if you are going to buy a new house, it is very difficult to find the house which meets feng shui requirements. And yet, you do not need to become pessimistic. Feng shui not only has ways to pull in good energy, but also it has ways to change negative energy into positive energy. Primarily, feng shui offers some ways of improvement by changing from bad to good energy; it is rare to find a house completely surrounded by negative energy.

There are two major methods for improving surroundings. First, determine where a dragon vein and a dragon hole are. Then you will call in good energy and let bad energy escape by using feng shui tools such as a feng shui compass. However, this is a territory of a feng shui master; if you want to do it on your own, you must study feng shui seriously.

Another method is "Do It Yourself feng shui." Many feng shui items will be introduced, and you can do it yourself using these feng shui items easily. There are more than 500 kinds of feng shui items, and energy is found in these items as they had been made by the people who had conceived and created a tool, and used it. When you display, place or hang genuine feng shui items created by traditional methods. It purifies the intrusion from the evil influence and activates good energy. When good connections are made, all fortune including wealth, love, business and such will improve.

This is called improving energy (Kasatsu koten) or eliminating evil energy (Kasatsu Fuusui.) This is the first feng shui step to improve feng shui. The study of feng shui has been around more than four thousand years, and we have inherited it. There are feng shui datum and knowledge based upon predecessors' experience. There is no way we should not use this valuable information to make our life better.

The purpose of feng shui is to take good care of our environment, and by going along with feng shui rules, we will obtain good luck. A sense of value in feng shui is gentle and this is in unity with the current trend of treating the earth gently. No wonder feng shui is getting a worldwide attention.

CHAPTER 1

☯

Indispensable Fundamental Feng Shui Items

THERE ARE MORE THAN 5000 FENG SHUI
ITEMS IN CHINA WHICH ARE HISTORI-
CALLY SUBSTANTIATED. BASIC FENG SHUI
ITEMS, THEIR USES, AND THEIR EFFECTS
ARE INTRODUCED IN THIS CHAPTER.

Feng Shui Compass (Luopan)

A feng shui master must have feng shui traditional tools. Among all the tools, the most important tool is a feng shui compass. Using all these tools, the feng shui master sees through invisible energy and put the living and business environment in order. When you can fully use the feng shui compass, you may consider yourself a feng shui master. At first, you might not understand what was written, but taking the feng shui compass in your hand is your first step. Soon you will realize that the world is moving according to the rule of feng shui.

Pertaining to cosmos and natural phenomena, there are all sorts of information including the theory of five elements (wood, fire, earth, metal and cold), Ba Gua Mirror, Yin and Yang, sexagenary cycle, positions of feng shui stars, changing seasons according to a lunar calendar on the feng shui compass. Although a feng shui master determines the best living and business locations and arranges the best furniture for them, that is not the only way to use a feng shui compass.

A feng shui compass controls the local energy and stabilizes the flow of energy. Even if the compass is not used, it can help remove evil spirits just by placing in the area where you feel uneasy or just by hanging on the wall of the front door or inside the room. Furthermore, energy will change to positive from negative if you are feeling negative and if the energy in the house seems to be negative.

In addition, when you carry the feng shui compass with you, calmness and peacefulness comes to you. It also minimizes the danger from a serious illness. Carrying a small feng shui compass as a charm is recommended.

A light malfunction affects the result
Feng Shui Compass

A feng shui Compass is a very precise tool. The impact, slight shift or severe jolting during transporting the compass tends to make its reading inaccurate. Moreover, there is the price change for the same product due to different methods of transportation. If the purpose of the compass is for an ordinary use, a general method of transportation is used. However, if it is meant for the use of a professional feng shui master, a professional carrier will very cautiously carry it with the carry-on luggage on the airplane.

There are two kinds of feng shui Compasses (Luopans.) There is an ultimate feng shui Compass (approximately over 26 cm [10 inches]) if you want to study feng shui seriously. There are ones with leveling tools. Sizes vary.

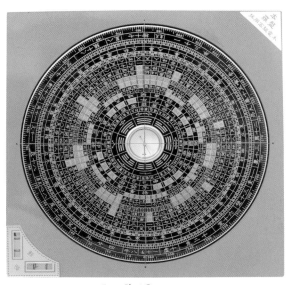

Feng Shui Compass

Suitable for beginners
Feng Shui Compass (Stable Compass)

A feng shui compass is the fundamental tool, but this particular compass is for the beginners who are not ready for more advanced feng shui. If it is not used, leave it in the living room etc., and it will alter energy.

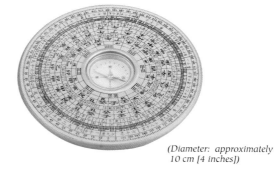

(Diameter: approximately 10 cm [4 inches])

For the prevention of traffic accidents and illness
Feng Shui Compass (with a carry on bag)

The official name is a small feng shui compass, and even if it is small, it is a genuine compass. It comes with a carrying bag, so it can be attached to the belt. It is said as you go out carrying it, you are likely to avoid traffic accidents and illness.

(Width: about 6 cm [2.5 inches])

Great product: marks both good and bad directions!
Transparent Feng Shui Compass

When this tool is placed on a map or a ground plan of the building, good and bad directions in the building may be judged. It is even better if it is used with an accurate directional magnet.

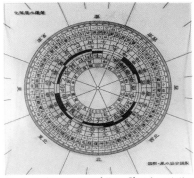

Product of International Feng Shui Association
(Width: approximately 15.5cm [6 inches]

To increase positive energy and stabilize atomosphere
Feng Shui Compass Wall Hanging

It is a hanging type of compass. Simply by hanging, it increases positive energy and stabilizes atmosphere. As it blocks negative energy, it is indispensable to hang on the bathroom door wall, places where water is used, and the front door. As it counteracts evil energy, it prevents bad energy if you place it in the northeastern direction and southwestern quarter of the building. When it is displayed in the car, it prevents traffic accidents.

It comes with Chinese style knotting decoration.

Stabilize energy disturbance
Feng Shui Energy Stabilizer

Good energy flows through space where the fung shui environment is in good order, and you feel safe and are able to live comfortably. However, it is unlikely that current houses and offices are equipped with a "perfect fung shui environment." Most buildings are bothered by energy disturbance or stagnation.

There are many fung shui goods which will improve environment by eliminating bad energy—specifically, a feng shui stabilizer that will control the disturbed energy in the affected area. Hanging it on the wall of the front door or keeping it in a room will stabilize the harmony of household.

This is an especially recommended item for improving relationships at home or a workplace. When there are constant arguments among family members or relationships among employees at a workplace, it would be a good idea to place an energy stabilizer in the area shared by many people. Gradually energy will be stabilized and a congenial atmosphere will return.

If there is a long corridor between the front door of a house and a room, or a telegraph pole is located in front of the

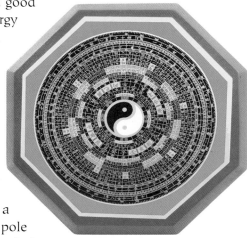

(Width: 17 cm [6.7 inches])

front door or an exit, it would be a good idea to use this item as it gets good results to avoid negativity and invite good luck.

As it also promotes the work of yin and yang, if you hope to see satisfactory results in your business, it is recommended to place it in a main room so that creative energy will be generated.

To measure length with good and bad fortune
Feng Shui Ruler (Luban Chi)

There are good and bad luck connected in directions. The feng shui compass is well known as a tool to measure good and bad luck for directions. The feng shui Ruler (officially called "Luban Chi") is used to determine length for its good or bad luck. In feng shui, it is believed that not only directions, but also length has lucky and unlucky measurements.

In China, feng shui rulers were used as an essential and unavoidable architectural tool. Not only used in Chinese architecture, but it is said that major buildings in the Heian period in Japan (8th – 12th centuries) were measured using feng shui rulers. Luban became a student of Zixiz, one of the ten disciples of Confucius, and discovered the good and bad fortune regarding the length. He is considered as God of Architecture in Taoism, and carpenters, carvers and such still believe in him even to the present day.

Unlike feng shui compass (Luopan), it is easy to use a feng shui ruler. By simply glancing at it, you can judge good and bad fortune of the length. As it is easy to use it in daily situations, it is a popular feng shui item.

First, let's measure your house, office, the entrance of

your shop (frontage and height.) If it is indicated by red, it indicates good fortune and it is a measurement of happiness. On the other hand, black will bring forth misfortune. You can feel safe if the measurement is red, but if it is black, it is best to change it to red. Having said that, it is not easy to rebuild it, but feel safe as it can be solved by switching the bad measurement to the made-believe good measurement. For instance, put decorative plants or shorten the frontage by hanging a curtain at the shop entrance. As simply changing the bad measurement to the good measurement, good energy will move into the building, and luck will increase.

There are specific areas that need to be measured using a feng shui ruler. Change them so that they will result in good measurement.

◆ **In the house:** a front door and the frontage and height of the entrance to the living room (measurement in the clear).

◆ **In the workplace (shop):** an entrance and exit where customers and employees use, the frontage and height of the front door, and the height of shelves where products are displayed.

*Feng Shui Measurement Tape (5cm [2 inches])
A feng shui ruler (Luban Chi) has been altered so that it is easy for modern people to use. The judgment of good or bad luck can be easily understood by the metric system.*

- **In the restaurant:** the height and the dimension of a chair, a table etc.
- **In the office, the parlor, and the managing director's room:** the frontage and height of the front door (height is most important.)

To measure length with good and bad fortune
Wooden Feng Shui Ruler (Luban Chi)

The origin of feng shui ruler is found here. It has been made after the prototype.

Feng Shui Ruler (Luban Chi)
(Length: 43cm, [16.9 inches] Made of wood)

Feng shui measurement ruler which improves bad fortune caused by measurement
Energy Improving
Feng Shui Measurement Ruler

When we arrange feng shui environment in a house, a store or office, there is a method of using a feng shui ruler and correct many building measurements to lucky measurement. However, a fact is that we cannot change all the bad fortune to good fortune using a feng shui measurement ruler. And yet, if we use an energy improving feng shui measurement ruler, we can change bad dimensions to good ones. All the bad measurements in the house will be erased, and only the good measurements will be left. At each end of measurements, yin and yang installed and bad fortune is changed to good fortune. It is best to install this product where most people pass by. If it is a house, it is usually installed on the front door. However, there are feng shui professionals who install this in the middle of the house. As it is effective for the entire area where it is installed, it is enough to place one ruler.

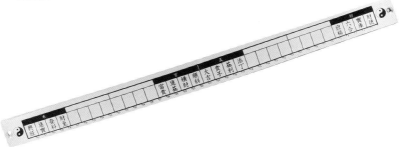

Improve all negative actions due to directions
Feng Shui Tile
to Improve Twelve Directions

This is the best feng shui item that prevents the invasion of evil spirits and stabilizes all the directions. It is well known that directions are regarded very important when various items are relocated or moved into a building. However, in modern society, it is often impossible to relocate our furniture to the best area in the building or actually move to another place. Some might say, "As I moved to a new place, my luck turned poor" or "a bathroom or a kitchen is in a bad direction in my house." It is said that your fortune will turn better as you simply hang this tile.

The meaning indicated by good and bad measurement

Measurement of good luck

Wealth	Prospering business, build up wealth, and harmonious home life
Wealth and Virtue	Blessed with wealth and virtue
Winning	Wins when you compete or gamble
Become rich	Able to gain wealth
Invites wealth	Invites wealth
Righteousness	Children devoted to parents are born
Prosperity of family	Family will prosper
Profit	Likely to gain profit
Precious child	Blessed with a precious child/children
Excellent luck	Everything will work for you.
Governmental work	Promotion, birth of a man of virtue
Getting good grades	Excellent examination results
Getting rich without trying	Getting rich without trying
Progress of studying	Progress of studying
Honor and wealth	Obtain Honor and wealth
Fortunate and lucky	Many good things come into your life
Get wealth	Become rich
Pass the examination	Success in an examination
Win in a lottery	Draw a winning ticket
Prosperity	Blessed with good family and prosperity

Measurement of bad luck

Illness	Frequent occurrence of illness and unfortunate events
Departure	Leave home, lose wealth
Flow	Wealth tends to flow away
Harm	Home will be harmed

There are times that you need to move to another place. For instance, your company asks you to transfer to another location, or you need to move your office or shop; and yet, your timing or moving directions are not ideal. When these situations occur, install a feng shui tile to improve twelve directions on the wall in the new place.

Feng Shui Basic Three Items

In feng shui, a good or bad direction and length are measured by a feng shui compass and feng shui ruler respectively. As a result, even if a partial bad luck sign appears, you cannot easily relocate or rebuild in reality. So, when we use a *feng shui measurement ruler* which improves bad fortune caused by measurement to good in length, a *feng shui tile to improve the twelve directions* from bad to good, and an *energy stabilizer* to stabilize surrounding energy, the Feng shui environment can be corrected. These three items are fundamental tools to eliminate bad energy in feng shui.

How to use Ba Gua and its effect

It is believed that an ideal topography for feng shui is a river in the east, a broad avenue in the west, a basin in the south, and a hill in the north. However, as every sort of tall building surrounds us, it is quite difficult to live in the ideal topography. Even if the inside of the building is arranged according to feng shui rules, negative energy might still result from the way the building is built or from nearby buildings. In order to protect from those obstacles, the knowledge of feng shui's purifying negative energy is indispensable.

As a method of purifying against evil, Ba Gua is well known. It is believed that Ba Gua drives away, bewitches and kills an atmosphere of malice. That is to say, Ba Gua has the power to keep away all that you do not want. According to The Book of Changes, Ba Gua refers to every direction (eight directions), eight seasonal changes (the first day of spring, vernal equinox, the first day of summer etc.), and eight seasonal winds, and it is considered as the best law for all things in nature and the movement of the cosmos.

The most common Ba Gua you see in Japan is a counterclockwise swastika as a Buddhist symbol. This was a Sanskrit character written on the chest of Buddha, and it shows all things in nature and the law of your own karma.

There are many items using Ba Gua, and it all depends on types of evils and circumstances. In any event, Ba Gua is a way to draw away negative energy and change for the better.

Solves the bad influence caused by geographical conditions
Ba Gua Mirror

Ba Gua Convex Mirror

It defends against maliciousness or evil spirits and scatters negative energy in a wide range of scope. Its characteristic is negative, and it should be placed in the following places as they tend to receive evil energy and declining fortunes.

◆ End of street
◆ Sharp object or the corner of the building that is facing you.
◆ There are two sharp buildings on both sides.
◆ Overpowering surrounding skyscrapers
◆ A junction of three roads in front of the building's entrance and exit
◆ A telegraph pole, a flagpole, a big tree etc. in front of the front door or the window.
  Place a Ba Gua convex mirror and keep yin and yang balance
◆ See many layered buildings.
◆ There is an elevator entrance and exit in the front of the building
◆ After you leave the front door in the building, there is an ascending stairway facing you.

When there are two sharp buildings on both sides of your building, place a ventilating fan next to a Ba Gua convex mirror on the roof or above the roof and run it; that way, negative energy will be blown away and become positive.

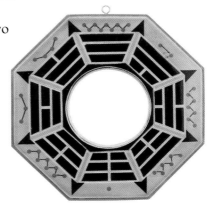

☯

Ba Gua Concave Mirror

As it collects light, it puts out negative energy and gets rid of it. Its characteristic is negative.

- ◆ After you leave the front door in the building, there is a descending stairway or a downhill road facing you.
- ◆ Your front door and the house in front of yours are facing each other.
- ◆ The building is outside of a road curve, a bridge, a river, a crossing with an overpass or an underpass etc.

    There are cases to install Ba Gua concave mirrors and expel bad energy.

- ◆ A large river drainage is running in front or by the side of a house or an office.

When good energy may escape because of the shape of property or a building, a Ba Gua concave mirror is used to recover it.

Because a Ba Gua Concave mirror reflects an image inversely, it has an effect of changing a bad thing into a good thing. There is another way of utilizing a Ba Gua concave mirror apart from chasing away bad energy. When there are good surroundings around buildings, a Ba Gua concave mirror might be used to take in a lot of good energy.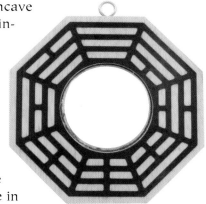

Flat Divination Mirror (Flat Ba Gua Mirror)

Collecting positive energy, it will reflect negative energy.

Place it in an unfavorable place or the area where yin and yang might be unbalanced and brings bad luck.

These are a cemetery, a funeral hall, a hospital, a Shinto shrine where a priest is not found.

Some parts of the house are missing.

The flat divination mirror may be used at the end of the street.

A flat Divination Mirror (Flat Ba Gua Mirror) is hung toward invading evil spirits. When a dragon or a lion's item is used in combination, its effect against eliminating evil becomes even more effective.

To keep away unpleasant things!
Energy Stabilizer with Ba Gua

The Ba Gua is added to the energy stabilizer mentioned in p. 18. This powerful item has double effects to stabilize energy in space and to keep away unpleasant things. Many unpleasant things happen in life. Even if it is not your fault,

you might be blamed. As a result, someone might be even stalking you. So, if you aren't happy with what's going on around you, the energy stabilizing Ba Gua may be what you need. You will avoid an unpleasant situation by using an energy stabilizing Ba Gua.

However, in comparison with the energy stabilizer, Ba Gua has weaker force for local stabilization. Hence, when the situation becomes calm, wrap the energy stabilizer with Ba Gua in black cloth, and change it to the energy stabilizer. When something unpleasant happens, change it to the energy stabilizer with Ba Gua. The trick is to choose correctly depending upon the situation. It further improves to keep distance of the unpleasant problem if you put a sward through a ginger together with other two methods noted above. (p. 109)

Prevents disasters and invites happiness
Ba Gua and Yin and Yang Stamp

Affixed on letters, envelopes, business cards and such, you will receive fortunate information. You will play an active part in your daily life as well as in business.

(Large: Height 6.2 cm [2.5 inches]
  Width 3.2 cm [1.2 inches])
(Medium: Height 6 cm [2.5 inches]
  Width 3.2cm [1.2 inches])
(Small: Height 6 cm [2.5 inches]
  Width 2.6 cm [1 inch])

Amulet for indoors
Copper Made Ba Gua and Yin and Yang Tile

Ba Gua has the power of purifying bloodthirsty atmospheres, containing distasteful things, and protecting you from evil. Yin and yang have the fundamental existence which composes all things. It has the power to create new things. When the two—Ba Gua, and yin and yang tiles, were combined, this has been used as various items from the ancient time.

Furthermore, as copper has a purifying effect against evil, the copper made Ba Gua and Yin and Yang tile a strong article to protect from evil. Hang it in directions, places or the front door where you feel uneasy about. Observe the house from the middle of your house. If placed around water, such as the bathroom, are located in a northeast or southwest direction in your house, it will protect from evil if you install it on the post and beam.

CHAPTER 2

Use the dragon's power to its maximum!

A DRAGON IS REGARDED AS SACRED
BEAST WITH MYSTERIOUS MAGICAL
POWER; SUCCESSIVE GENERATIONS OF
EMPERORS SPECIALLY TREATED IT WITH
DIGNITY. THE POWER THAT COMES
FROM A DRAGON IS INDISPENSABLE TO
ADJUST THE FENG SHUI ENVIRONMENT.

To obtain the location with right energy movement

When you build a building, we give serious considera-
tion to whether the building site has good or bad energy in feng shui. For good topography, good energy will
flow and good fortune will be found. It is said that you will
prosper if you live there.

Based upon the cosmic dual forces (yin and yang) and
the five elements (metal, wood, water, fire and earth) in Chinese cosmology, the best location has four protective gods.
An Azure Dragon, a White Tiger, a Vermilion Bird, and a
Black Tortoise protect east, west, south and north respectively. In addition, there are kochin and tooda in the middle
the location where yin and yang are indicated.

To be specific, there are mountains and hills in north and
rivers that flow to the east. There are oceans and ponds
while spacious plains expand in south, and big roads go
through in west. The best energy flows through the passage,
and good water, which means river and roads, activates energy. Sand, which means mountains and hills, guards energy which was collected where it congregates. The area is
considered to be the best place to establish a palace and the
capital. The locations of ancient Nara, ancient Kyoto and
Edo, which all prospered for a long time, were chosen based
upon this theory.

Nevertheless, it is almost impossible to request a good
location, as noted above, in modern society; so four protective Taoist gods help improve environmental imperfection
The pictures and ornaments of these four gods not only
change the aspect of a location but they are also believed to

improve and grow your fortune by making money. So, it is important to be assertive in using of items representing these gods and bring their power into a house, an office and a store. You will then formulate an ideal topography for the four Taoist gods in feng shui and will become prosperous.

How a dragon was treated in Feng Shui

There are four gods and a number of lucky animals in feng shui. Most of them are imaginary beasts. A dragon has a special place in feng shui. I will state reasons later, but the dragon is considered a sacred animal. Even though it does not exist in reality, knowledge of dragons has been handed down from generation to generation through oral tradition throughout the world; indeed, it is a mysterious animal. A dragon is regarded as a god in Japan, and many other countries in Asia symbolize a dragon as a god as well. On the other hand, a dragon symbolizes evil in the west but generates immense interest.

In feng shui, a dragon protects the east as one of the four Taoist gods and is respected as a "Azure Dragon" to bring in fortune and success in your life. However, the Chinese people had admired a dragon even before feng shui was established, and the dragon was dealt with carefully. Dragons are so dear to them that Chinese call themselves as "descendants of dragons."

Buddhist scriptures in ancient India consider a dragon as one of eight kinds of sacred beings which are beasts with a human face and a beast body: heaven, dragon, yaksha, Kendappa, Asura, Garuda, Kimnara, Makraka. In China, however, a dragon has nine features: a horn is of a deer, a head is of a camel, an ear is of a cow, eyes are of a hare, a nape of the neck (a torso) is of a snake, a stomach is of mizura (an imaginary snake like animal), scales are of a carp, nails are of hawk, and hands are like of a tiger.

The characteristics of the dragon are long whiskers at its mouth and scales grown inversely under its throat. According to Han Feizi, the dragon brings wrath down upon the person who touched the scales, and even death might occur. Touching (a dragon's) scale means to make someone very angry in Japanese language.

Only the dragons have ranks, and a number of claws show a certain ranks. Five claws are allowed only for the Emperors, four claws are allowed only for temples, shrines and mausoleum, and three claws are allowed for common people. That is to say, the more claws it has, the higher the rank is.

This rule was established after the Song dynasty. It meant to raise the Emperor's authority by limiting the use of dragons. Afterwards, a dragon became a symbol of an Emperor; by deciding the ranks of dragons by a number of claws, the commoners were allowed to worship dragons. This proves how special dragons are.

As stated in the beginning, a dragon is a sacred beast that plays a special role. That is because all the energy on the ground equal dragons. As indicated by a proverb "Life is in the earth; the earth gives birth to all things," the energy born in the earth is the origin of life. The origin—which is a dragon—has immeasurable strength. Furthermore, it creates a good omen and has power of influencing energy. Because of these reasons, a feng shui master looks for a dragon vein.

Good energy lives on the dragon vein, and it circulates following its flow. Incidentally, a mountain range is often synonymous to a dragon vein. It is due to the fact that dragons remind of a curvy mountain range, and people have worshiped both mountain ranges and dragons.

A feng shui master's role is to thoroughly observe dragons and arrange the environment for dragons. It is the feng shui master's ability to handle a dragon as it can be a friend or a foe.

While using the power of a dragon, the use of water cannot be forgotten. The dragon usually lives underwater, but it ascends to the sky in spring. In fall, it again lies low deep in the water. So, the dragon administers all the water on the ground, and it controls rain freely.

It is said that if there is water, there is a dragon; there is a very strong relationship between dragons and water. As dragons are a creature that obtains strength by water power, so if the dragon's strength is needed with wind and water, the use of water becomes extremely important.

Make sure that you understand the characteristics of a dragon, and use it carefully. Then dragons will definitely bring happiness.

A goblet that invites prosperity
A Good Fortune Cupper Goblet

This is a goblet to offer water to a dragon. A dragon requires water, and when the water is offered, the dragon's power increases. Place the goblet filled with fresh water near the dragon's mouth—you need to change the water daily. Once you do it, the dragon starts to become very active, and various situations will be corrected with positive energy.

Furthermore, a message inviting prosperity is written on the goblet, so you can expect your monetary fortune to improve. Where some water is left in the goblet, do not throw it away. It can be scattered about the front door or given to plants. Incidentally, if no water is found in the goblet, it simply becomes an ornament. It won't do any harm.

Kinds of Dragons and Benefit

We previously stated that a dragon was energy itself. As energy has been thought to give birth to everything, every animal in China is born from a dragon. For instance, Hiryuu (flying tiger) gave birth to a firebird goddess, and she in return gave birth to a falcon. Then the falcon gave birth to all animals with wings. Ooryu (a dragon with a pair of wings) gave birth to kenba, and she gave birth to kirin (Chinese unicorn). Kirin gave birth to all the beasts.

Koryu (a dragon with scales on its body) gave birth to Kon, and she gave birth to Kenjya. Kenjya gave birth to all living things with scales. Senryuu gave birth to gen (a large sea turtle), and she gave birth to reiki, and she gave birth to all things with shells. Several names of dragon have been mentioned, but there are various kinds of dragons from which appearance and characteristics are different. Dragons are classified in accordance with their appearances, characteristics, and abilities. The main dragons are listed as follows:

Classified by appearance
- **Koryu**: a dragon with scales on its body.
- **Ooryu**: a dragon with a pair of wings.
- **Hanryu**: a dragon which coiled its tail prior to flying to the sky.
- **Kyuryu**: a dragon with a horn or horns on its head.
- **Chiryu**: a dragon without a horn or horns on its head.

Classified by characters
- **Seiryu**: a dragon in favor of water.
- **Karyu**: a dragon in favor of fire.
- **Nakiryu**: a dragon which is good at roaring.
- **Sekiryu**: a warlike dragon.

Classified by abilities
- **Tenryu**: a dragon with overall abilities granted by heaven;its power gushes out from its inside.
- **Shinryu**: a dragon having abilities to make wind blow and to rain fall.
- **Chiryu**: a dragon having abilities to administer all the source of river such as lakes and springs.
- **Gohouzouryu**: a dragon having abilities to protect special treasured items.

Dragons are said to hold various powers—especially those dragons that have noble characters have special power to invite noblemen. When you encounter with difficulties and need some help, it is said a dragon will bring you a nobleman who will give you a clue to solve the problem. Because of the nobleman's power, it will also solve the troubles among people. Needless to say, the dragon only helps when the person faced with problems are doing their best.

It also symbolizes wealth and auspiciousness, so it invites riches, and especially, it is well known to purify wickedness. Wickedness comes from many places. For instance, you will find wickedness around a cemetery where the thirst for blood exists. Also, you will find wickedness in places where many people come and go, or the building standing next to the police station or the temple is affected by wickedness. Likewise, if the corner of the building faces these directions, it is affected by wickedness. The wickedness caused by them is solved by counteraction produced by dragons.

Specific ways to use dragon goods are introduced now.

How to Use
Dragon Goods Correctly

When you use the dragon feng shui items skillfully, the strong power of dragons can be applied. The correct area to place a dragon ornament is right to the front door or a room. It may also face north. By doing so, it will call in a good dragon; it will gain auspiciousness and wealth and your quest for love will improve.

The reason to place a dragon in the right side is relating to the energy of yin and yang. It is said that a dragon feels more comfortable placed in the right side. North is the direction of water. As a dragon seeks water, water makes dragons become more active. Even if you place the ornament in incorrect places, there is nothing to worry about. It becomes a regular ornament, and it will not harm you. However, there are areas a dragon dislikes. As a dragon is a creature of water, there is a compatibility issue if it is placed on a television, a computer, a refrigerator and such.

A dragon does not like an alcove. It is a sacred place where noble people sit. If necessary, you will need to place a five-fingered dragon that serves only the Emperor.

It may also be placed in the east. That happens when the power of energy in the west is stronger than the east. As explained for the section of an ideal topography for the four Taoist gods, each direction has a certain meaning in feng shui. A position of the Azure Dragon in the east is a place reserved for a nobleman, and it is an auspicious place inviting assistance from friends and colleagues. On the contrary, the White Tiger is a position for an unimportant person, and a bad position causing fights. It is important to strengthen the dragon power in the house in order to weaken a tiger's coercion so that we can live peacefully among each other. By doing so, a dragon will invite a noble man and acquire his help. If the White Tiger's energy wins, troubles among people may increase.

If the room in which you spend for a considerable time a day is located in the west, or the east of the room is dark and energy is weak, you need to put a tiger ornament made of copper, a tiger picture and a wall hanging in the east which is a position for the Azure Dragon. By doing so, it alters the balance of power with the White Tiger.

Keeping things tidy and in order in a room is important so that a dragon can live comfortably there. Even if a dragon ornament invites a dragon to come in, it will not stay if not comfortable. It is especially important to keep water-related areas such as a kitchen and a bathroom clean. If they are dirty, the dragon, which likes water, will leave.

You need to offer one clean bowl of water per day. If you would be away for the duration, you need give a lot of water in a larger dish. If the amount of water decreases because the dragon starts drinking water, it is proof that that your fortune is ascending.

Lastly, if you use a dragon ornament, there is one thing you must bear in mind. You must choose the dragon that you are pleased with, and take care of it with love as if it were your pet. If it gets dirty a little bit, clean it with gentle cloth. When you give water, say "Good morning." You can say anything you like to talk about to the dragon; it could be about your worries or dreams. The dragon will listen to you wholeheartedly. Your dragon will become very active, and it should bring you good luck.

Note: Because dragons are most exemplary Feng shu igoods, there are many counterfeits. It is important you buy a genuine article.

Every fortune will turn for the better
Feng Shui Sansuiryu

Sansuiryu, a dragon that has descended hills and waters and tried to grab a crystal ball, is the most powerful and high ranked dragon among many dragons. When the most powerful and graceful dragon serving the Emperor is placed in your office, your store or your house, it will descend the dragon passage and brings fortune. Furthermore, as crystal purifies evil spirits and it will become a dragon ball. It then will increase the dragon's power. Feng shui will change negative energy to positive energy.

However, it is very important to offer fresh water to the dragon. The dragon is connected to water, so place fresh water in a container and put it near the dragon's lips. Then, the water will provide the dragon energy, and the dragon will grant your wishes, desires and dreams. If the water level lowers, it is the proof that luck is coming your way. In addition, the water placed near the dragon's mouth helps to create a hole which is a spot where the dragon's energy accumulates. Sansuiryu looks solid, and it is a major product representing dragon items.

(Height: 36.5cm [14 inches])

Wish for it and fortune will turn for the better
Five Fingered Wishing Dragon

A powerful stone can be placed on the palm of a five fingered wishing dragon. If your luck is down and want to improve it, or you have a special wish, place a crystal ball. If you want your love life or human relationship improve, place a rose quartz ball. If you want to be richer, place a gold rutile or a tiger's eye. When you place these stones, you must make your wishes sincerely. If you use a wooden pedestal, you can line up and place a number of these stones there.

It is best to place a tiger on the right after entering the front door or a room. Giving fresh water every day in a bowl and placing it near the dragon's mouth, you will take care of it with affection as if it were your pet, and it will become active rapidly in order to meet your wishes. It is a good idea to place a crystal ball with water in it; it will improve the dragon's power. The water in the crystal ball which has been receiving natural energy from ancient times will pass its energy to the dragon.

Your desires are granted due to the synergistic effect of seven positions of crystals

Ascending Dragon with Seven Positioned Crystal Balls

(Container for good luck and feng shui items)

Only the Emperor in China was permitted to use the five fingered dragon, and this is a tall container with the five fingered dragon wrapped around the column. The inside of the tall container is hollow, and you place important items that you want your wishes granted. For instance, they are a lottery ticket, a betting ticket on a horse, an admission ticket for an examination, a registered seal, jewelry, medicine, a picture of either your girl friend or boy friend, and your own picture when you were thinner. The combined power of the dragon and seven positioned crystals will grant your wishes. Incidentally, if some items such as a stock certificate and a pass book do not fit in the container, it would be best to place them under the container.

(Height: about 19.5 cm [7.7 inches])

The lid on the container describes "seven positioned crystal balls", and there are spaces provided to place one crystal ball in the center and six crystal balls around the

☯

perimeter. The crystal ball placed in the center is a dragon ball of the ascending dragon wrapping around the column. Its characteristic is to double and triple the power of the dragon. The best place to place it is to the right of the front door or you should place it to the right side of the living room or your own room.

There are various ways to handle the "ascending dragon with seven positioned crystal balls", and they are as follows:

◆ Fill one-third of the container with fresh water. Then place natural crystal on "seven positioned crystal balls" described on the container lid. Change the water once a day. A dragon offered fresh water will become active even more.

◆ Do not pour water into the hollow of the tall container, but use it to keep items relating to money matters. For instance, you might like to keep your lottery ticket until the drawing date or keep your registered seal. It would be best to pour water in a good luck goblet made of copper and place it near the tall container.

◆ There is a hook where you can hang a necklace in the back of the lid. By placing valuable jewelry, the power of that stone will be further activated.

Bring in so much luck that you cannot stop laughing!
Laughing Dragon (Made of Copper)

It is an unusual dragon as if it were laughing very hard. Since good fortune and happiness will come to the home of those who smile, a laughing dragon symbolizes good fortune. In addition to the dragon's various power, it brings smiles to you and your life. Holding a natural crystal on its hand, it adds the crystal power to help materialize your wishes. It would be better to place it where your family would meet such as a living room. The dragon will cherish its power so that each of the family members will be healthy and live each life happily. When a good thing happens, talk to the dragon, and laugh together. The dragon will be so happy that it will work harder for you, and it will fill up the house with happiness.

(Height: 17cm [7 inches])

Prevents evil spirits and luck will improve!
Feng Shui Dragon (Made of Copper)
– Golden Color
Feng Shui Dragon (Made of Copper)
– Old Copper Color

Among feng shui items that produce "the route of energy", the dragon vein, and bring in good luck, the most fundamental item is a feng shui dragon. Basically, it is placed in the room, and just by doing so, it prevents the evil spirit from coming to you. Good energy comes through a flowing body of the dragon, and it will bring all of luck. It is very effective to obtain a competitive edge in business or increase your personal fortune. If you want to utilize the power of this dragon, it is best to place it near water. You should place it to the right of or on the top of a water tank, or place the dragon's head toward the direction of an ocean, a river or a pool. If it is not feasible, pour fresh water in a small container and place it next to the dragon's mouth. In accordance with the study of feng shui, place the dragon toward north, a direction of "water", and your monetary fortune will turn better. Whether choosing gold or old copper is up to

Old copper (Large)
(26cm [10.2 inches])

you; you need to choose whichever the color you will be affectionate for the item for a long time.

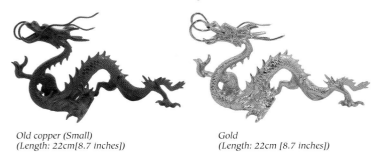

Old copper (Small)
(Length: 22cm[8.7 inches])

Gold
(Length: 22cm [8.7 inches])

Powerful Yin and Yang effect
A Pair of Male and Female Dragon Ornament

A pair of male and female dragon ornaments increases
the energy of a dragon to its maximum because of the yin
and yang effect, and it helps produce new things as well.
Furthermore, as both dragons face each other, powerful positive energy is collected between two dragons. It is said that
the energy brings good luck to people around them and in
surrounding environment. It is an essential feng shui item
for overseas Chinese merchants. It is thick and heavy and
made of pure brass.

Powerful Yin and Yang effect
A Wall Ornament with a Set of Three Items

A wall ornament with a set of two dragons and a dragon ball (fire ball) is most appropriate to increase business fortune. A pair of dragons facing each other is a lucky item; your fate will go to the heaven (lucky) riding on a dragon, and it is easy to install. There is also a set of dragons representing yin and yang with the mystical firebird goodness.

*Dragon and dragon
(Length: 42.2cm each
[16.6 inches])*

Wall hanging dragon item
Dragon Disk and Mystical Firebird Goodness Disk

A dragon disk is a feng shui item that calls wealth and luck in. Just by hanging the disk, the power of wealth and luck chases evil away and brings

*Dragon and Mystical Firebird Goodness Disk:
(Large: 29cm [11.4 inches])
(Small: 23 cm [9 inches])*

fate up. Even if there is no space to place an ornament, it can be easily decorated. "The dragon disk and the mystical firebird goodness disk" has power to summon things. It is effective for new encounters and the development of business.

Dragon Disk
(Diameter: 27.5cm [10.0 inches])

Reliable presence bringing in the best luck
The Five Fingered Dragon Holding up a Dragon Ball Powerfully

The five fingered dragon holding up a dragon ball powerfully is a reliable presence for those whom you like to give good fortune. The more you treat it affectionately, the better it will move the stagnating air and bring better fortune.

Large: (Height: approximately 32cm [13 inches])
Small: (Height: approximately 20cm [8 inches])

See Powerful Yin and Yang Effect
Double Dragons of Toryusenki

A pair of dragons ascends from the mountain wizard road. The way two five fingered dragons are entangled is regarded as bringing much luck ever since the ancient times.

The two dragons contain the power of yin and yang, and they collect all the energies available in the area; then they produce a new power spot. The crystal held in both hands of dragons turns into dragon balls and gather energy; the energies of dragons and crystal form a harmonious whole, give limitless power, and increase power. Thus, it will bring you wonderful fortune.

We recommend the double dragons for those people who want to increase the luck of business as well as at home or the luck of finance as well as love. It is also highly recommended for a business proprietor who has established two business undertakings at the same time.

Name the dragons and treat them with love.

(Height: approximately 19 cm) [7.5 inches])

Invites happiness, auspiciousness and good fortune
A Pot that Feng Shui Water Moves

This feng shui pot produces a dragon hole into which a dragon flies down. It is a mysterious pot; pouring water into this brass pot and rub the brass handles, the water in the pot will start to move and spray with the cry of dragon. The spray is to be believed the proof of dragon's moving in and out. As you move the water artificially and create a dragon hole, you are calling "happiness, auspiciousness and good fortune" in. This is a treasured item secretly cherished by successive Chinese Emperors.

(Diameter: approximately
38.5cm [15 inches]
Height: approximately
12.5cm [5 inches])

A dragon runs about the heavens and the earth
Ornament Illuminating the Energy of Heavens and the Earth to Your Treasure

Three fundamental rules of feng shui are acknowledging the time of the heavens, obtaining the benefit of the earth, and attempting harmony among people. While following the heavens, the earth produces all things. It changes according to the heavens' rules. The dragon in the ornament symbolizes energy that runs through the dragon's vein.

When you rotate the ornament, it raises the energy of the heavens and activates through the energy of the earth (dragon vein). As a human hand moves it lastly, three fundamental rules of feng shui are put in order.

(Height: approximately 33 cm [13 inches])

The first step to better fortune!
A Dragon Holding a Crystal Ball

This is a small dragon ornament, and it is best suited when there is not enough space to display a bigger ornament. A five fingered dragon is a symbol specifically

Small: Made of copper with 20mm [8 inches] natural crystal
Dragon: (Height: approximately 5cm [2 inches])
Pedestal: (Height: approximately 2cm [0.8 inches])

for an Emperor. The inside of "the dragon holding a crystal ball" is hollow, and a 20mm crystal ball can be installed. The combined effect of a dragon and a crystal ball could be expected. This is the feng shui item if you want to improve your fortune for the first time.

Crystal has extremely high ability to cleanse the area where it is placed. The energy surrounding the area is cleansed, and negative energy will be changed to positive energy. By placing this crystal ball inside, the dragon's power will further increase, and it will bring good fortune more and more.

As a dragon likes water, pour fresh water in the water bowl and place it near the dragon. When water is not available, crystal pebbles may be used. Place it in the front door or right to the room. If not applicable, there is no problem to put it anywhere you like. However, be careful not to place it near electric appliances because full ability cannot be exhibited.

Large: Made of copper with 20mm
[8 inches] natural crystal
Dragon: (Height: approximately 8cm [3 inches])
Pedestal: (Height: approximately 2cm [0.8 inches])

CHAPTER 3

☯

Get hold of powerful fortune with the power of animals

MANY ANIMALS BESIDES DRAGONS AP-
PEAR IN FUNG SHUI, AND IT SURPRISES
US THAT SOME ANIMALS HOLD UNEX-
PECTED POWER. THIS CHAPTER INTRO-
DUCES THE MEANING AND EFFECT EACH
ANIMAL HOLDS. APPLY THE POWER OF
ANIMALS AND GET HOLD OF POWERFUL
FORTUNE.

Have the best Feng Shui environment in your room

Are you familiar with Kitora tomb in Nara prefecture which was created in the end of 7th century and the beginning of 8th century? From a recent study, we have found out that there are Vermilion Bird, Black Tortoise, Azure Dragon, and White Tiger on the south, the north, the east and west walls respectively. The sun, the moon and the astronomical pictures were drawn on the ceiling. The reason for the four gods to be placed so is to arrange the balance of yin and yang so that "energy" is activated.

To share the good luck of this example, we like to take in the power of the four gods. First, look at the floor plan of your house. If it is not available, you might like to draw a rough sketch on your own. A balcony may be ignored. First, you mark the center of the house. Next, you mark the east, the west, the south and the north in your house. Following the way Kitora tomb was founded, place Vermilion Bird in the south, Black Tortoise in the north, Azure Dragon in the east, and White Tiger in the west.

Placing the four gods in proper locations, and by doing so, you will have an ideal topography for the four Taoist gods. After you arrange the feng shui environment in order and create your own fortune, all the fortune including health, wealth, and human relations will turn for the better.

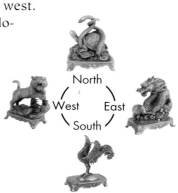

North

West   East

South

White Tiger

F rom ancient times, humans were afraid of tigers while respecting its overpowering strength and courage. In feng shui, White Tiger protects west, and it is the only savage secret beast among four secret beasts, Azure Dragon, Vermillion bird, White Tiger and Black Tortoise. It might harm human relations if White Tiger is used incorrectly, so it must be used with care.

Nevertheless, it is not always a savage beast. A proverb says, "Fight one evil with another." Because the tiger has authoritative attitudes, it is said to change fortune for the better. In feng shui, the overbearing frightening quality of a tiger is utilized as it cleanses evil and negative energy. When powerful negative energy is invading from outside, the tiger will take an active role and remove the negative energy.

A tiger ornament is to be placed to the right side of your own seat, so the person who is facing you may assume that you are used to tame a tiger. It is also commonly done that you keep the tiger in the front door of your house or an office so that it may be function as a security guard. By doing so, not only preventing the entry of evil spirit, it can transfer authority and combative spirit to yourself. Because of that, if leadership is needed, this is the most appropriate feng shui animal. There is a word of caution; if the power of a tiger is stronger than a dragon, human relationships could become harmful, so place a tiger ornament, and keep things balanced.

Conquer your rival
White Tiger Ornament

Because a tiger loves solitude, it is said that it might harm human relations. On the other hand, it is affectionate toward a spouse and cubs. When you place a tiger ornament in a common space of your house such as the front door or a living room, it improves the relationship among parents and children as well as general human relationship.

However, please avoid displaying the tiger in a bedroom or individuals' rooms as it changes itself to a vicious animal. The place you might display is toward west when looking from the center of the house (or from the room), or put it toward the left when looking from the front door. Incidentally, it is standard to put a dragon ornament on the right when looking from the front door to the inside of the house.

If tiger eye is the material the tiger is sculptured, the power to repel evil energy becomes intensified. This is recommended for those who want to increase wealth and business fortune, or start up a business and a new project, or want to conquer a rival.

Black Tortoise

This sacred beast is an imaginary creature and is called Black Tortoise. It symbolizes a snake which entangles with a turtle. Primarily, Black Tortoise rules over the northern heavens of twenty-eight mansions of Chinese astronomy (constellations dividing the ecliptic into 28 positions.)

Ancient Chinese thought that the earth of which four ends were slightly raised held the sky of hemisphere. In fact, Black Tortoise symbolizes the universe. A shell symbolizes the heaven, and an abdomen symbolizes the earth. The snake wrapped around the tortoise symbolizes the water which freely circulates and the atmosphere freely floats between the heavens and the earth.

In feng shui, Black Tortoise is a sacred beast protecting northern territory, and it plays a role of protection from the attack of the enemy from behind. That is why, the Emperor of China sets with his back facing north; it was said that two ornaments of a turtle and a snake were placed in that manner.

The reason that Black Tortoise has a strange figure is based on an anecdote of Taoism. The stomach of Black Tortoise changed its shape to a turtle, and his intestines changed its shape to a snake. In Taoism, Black Tortoise is respected as one of the top gods. People still believe in him even today: if one is possessed by an evil spirit, he or she will ask Black Tortoise to purify it, or he or she will ask Black Tortoise to protect from an unexpected attack.

Protect in the rear!
Copper Black Tortoise Ornament

This Black Tortoise ornament protects northward. If you place it in the farthest place seeing from the northern direction or the front door, it becomes a guardian deity to purify from evil spirit and protect from negativity.

Because it protects the back, if it is placed behind the company president's desk or the seat behind his or her library, business will conduct smoothly, and the competition against business rivals will be advantageous. It also protects from negativity while doing research and study.

As north is in the direction of water in the five elements of traditional Chinese philosophy, it can be placed where a fire can easily start such as in a warehouse where a lot of papers are kept.

(Height: approximately 7.5 cm [3 inches])

Vermilion Bird

In the five elements of traditional Chinese philosophy, beautiful Vermilion Bird is a sacred bird to protect the southern heavens. As it symbolizes summer, it is also called Phoenix.

A Method to Produce an Ideal Topography for the Four Taoist Gods

Ever since the ancient time, it has been said that it would be best for the Emperor, the head of the family and an elder in the family to sit facing the south in Chinese cultural sphere, and the same theory has been passed down to Japan. In the Edo Period, it was said that a samurai sat facing the south.

As the head of the family sits facing the south, Vermilion Bird sitting in the south looks ahead, gathers information regarding future prospects and tells the master. Vicious and yet tamed, White Tiger sits next to his master's right facing the west. To the left of the master, Azure Dragon, which improves the master's fortune, is placed. Finally, in order to protect a sudden attack in the rear, Black Tortoise whose carapace is regarded as a mountain is placed in the north. Furthermore, the master sits in the middle where yin and young are mixed and the atmosphere is most active. These are the strongest positions for both attack and defense. This is how an ideal topography for the four Taoist gods.

There are two ways to formulate an ideal topography. As shown in the picture A, property is considered from surround-

Phoenix sits in the forefront among the four gods and look out over faraway places from the high place. In other words, it has the ability to collect information and has the accurate ability to see the future. Because of this reason, it is said to offer the front space so that Vermilion Bird can fly away

ings. On the other hand, property is considered from within as shown in the picture B. Anyone can formulate an ideal topography making using of the picture B. In this method, you stand in the center of the room and regard the main entrance and exit as the south. Therefore, the right is the location of White Tiger in the west, the left is the location of Azure Dragon in the east, and the opposite of the entrance and exist is Black Tortoise in the north. That is to say, imagine yourself getting into this room. You place Azure Dragon on the right, White Tiger on the left, Black Tortoise in the inner section of the room that is away from the entrance and exist, and Vermillion Bird near the entrance and the exit door. By placing four Taoist gods in this manner, you can produce the ideal feng shui topography for your own house or a room.

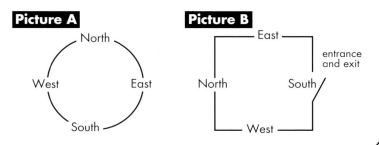

Picture A

North
West
East
South

Picture B

East
entrance and exit
North
South
West

easily. Unfortunately, among imaginary animals and beasts, there is little written about it, there are little pictures of Vermilion Bird, and a figure of Vermilion Bird is rather mysterious.

Lion

The lion is the king of the beasts, and it also represents an auspicious beast in feng shui. There is always a pair of large lions next to both sides of the main gates in traditional palaces and official buildings in China. They represent dignity and nonaggression. There are many animals possessing the power of protection from the evil spirit; and yet, the power of a lion is immense.

Lions offer two effects: the first is to increase business fortune and invite wealth, and the second is to draw evil spirit away. As far as business fortune and inviting wealth are concerned, it will increase the fortune of a room or a building where a lion is placed. It makes no difference in which direction the lion is placed, but it is common to place it near the front door. When there is a passage between the front and back doors, or there are many doors in the store, there is in the danger of too much a flow of energy, and wealth might escape through the flow of energy. As for the effect of purifying negative energy, a lion has immense power. It is an indispensable feng shui ornament. For this purpose, it is important that the lion must face outside.

In Chinese, a lion is pronounced as "siizu". In Okinawan "schiesser", it is said that the lion culture was imported from China, and "schiesser" was mispronounced from "siizu." Hence, the purpose of using a "schiesser" is almost the same as using a lion ornament in China.

When one item of a pair of feng shui item is damaged, you need to exchange both of the pair.

Shutting out the entrance of evil
Feng Shui Lion

The power of protection against evil by lions is immense. A pair of male and female lion figures protects the front door of the house, and all the evil spirits are shut out to enter into the house. Especially when the front door faces the end of the street, negative energy directly hits and it is bad luck. In this case, it is important to place a pair of lions by the front door for the purpose of drawing out evil energy.

A dragon is placed inside the room, but lions display the protective power against evil when put outside of the room. So, placing them at the front door facing outside is important. It is a custom to place a male on the left and a female on the right of which their backs are facing the front door. This is based upon the teaching of the yin and yang, which specifies to place Azure Dragon on the left and White Tiger on the right.

The effect of lions is not limited to the protection from evil, but its power to invite wealth is immense. Hence, this is the best feng shui animal if you are wishing for prosperous business.

▌ *Purify evil spirit by strong power!*
Lion Made of Copper Tile

This tile lion is as effective to purify evil spirits as a lion ornament. In case a pair of a male and female lion pair ornament is not available, this item often may be replaced. The lion's face is powerful and strong power is gathered as eyes are wide open, Yin and yang and the Ba Gua are on its forehead, and seven star swords are held in its mouth. Hang the tile lion on both sides of front door or paste it on the wall.

It is especially useful to draw away the evil spirit coming toward you. An example is that the corner of the wall or the corner of the roof opposite of your house is facing (coming to) you. Another example is that there is a front door in front of an elevator, and the evil spirit is coming toward you. Place the tile lion facing the evil spirit.

Unlike a tiger, it does not harm people, so it can be used easily at home or at work.

Stops negative, evil and ghostly energies
Copper Ba Gua Lion Tile

You utilize this item when you cannot place a lion ornament just as in the case of a lion tile. A yin and yang Ba Gua
sign is engraved on its forehead, and it holds a seven star
sword in its mouth. By placing each of this on the front door
or both sides of entrance and exit, it stops invisible negative
evil and ghostly energy. It also works to avoid bad energy
when you place it in a dark room or place that tends to di-
minish fortune.

Horse

A horse is not a sacred beast, but it is an indispensable and familiar animal for nomadic people who required horses for daily living. A horse symbolizes strong life forces, and it invites wealth and increases business fortune. In order to increase wealth, it is important to place in the correct place. It has to be placed due south, a position of the Horse in the twelve horary signs.

Since a horse was an important means of transportation, it represents movement and relocation. Regarding this point, a horse other than any other feng shui animals is most effective. It is very useful for a move, a transfer, studying abroad, further education, getting a job, a reshuffling of personnel, changing a job, opening business, drawing lots for apartment and condominium complexes. In these instances, place a horse where the northern wall (a Black Tortoise wall) and the western wall (a White Tiger wall) meet.

The most important thing at this point is which direction a horse's face should be faced. When you have a clear objective such as a move or studying abroad, make sure that you face the horse's face toward that direction. It is necessary to use a feng shui compass, magnet to indicate directions, and a map so that it is accurate. If you don't have a clear objective yet, it is not necessary to think about to which direction the horse face should face.

A horse is not a sacred beast, so you should not place it with such ferocious beasts as a lion and a tiger. You should put them separately as much as you can so they can't see each other.

Materialize move or change
Feng Shui Horse Ornament Made of Copper

A feng shui horse ornament made of copper is an indispensable item when you are relocating. If you want to look for the most appropriate location to move, place the horse ornament in the front door of where you live or your store. It is better to put the horse's head facing outside.

In case your move is decided, bring the horse ornament there. Place the horse's head facing the indoor more than three days, and then you will move in. After your move is finished and you have completely settled down, move the horse ornament to the south. It will work for prosperity and normalize family relationship.

(Height: approximately 20cm [8 inches] made of copper.)

Chinese Unicorn

An imaginary animal known in China from the ancient time is said to be a congratulatory animal for auspicious benevolence. When a great Emperor rules the world, a Chinese unicorn is said to appear in order to celebrate.

The general picture of Chinese unicorn is as follows: it resembles a deer but is bigger than a deer. A hoof resembles that of a horse, and its tail resembles that of a cow. A whole body is covered with fish scales, and it has a horn or two horns on its head. Both male and female Chinese unicorns have the same shape. In its Chinese character, 麒 means a male, and 麟 means a female. In China, the symbol of an Emperor was a dragon, that of an Empress was mythical fire-bird goddess, and that of a naval or a military officer was a Chinese unicorn. As it is bright and respects justice, the Chinese unicorn is also called as a benevolent animal.

In China, an outstanding child is spoken figuratively as a Chinese unicorn. There is a Chinese phrase about a promising child; it is well known that such a child is dignified, gentle, and mature. Furthermore, the voice of the child is so beautiful that people think they are listening to music.

A Chinese unicorn has a power of suppression, so it overpowers all troubles and stabilizes energy in the area. It is an item to eradicate bad energy. It improves unstable income (bankruptcy), friction at home, the relationship between couples, and human troubles in business; that is to say, it helps to overpower all the problems we face

A Chinese unicorn is a symbol to protect peace. As we live in the troublesome world, it is highly recommended to decorate your room with the Chinese unicorn.

Solves all troubles
Chinese Unicorn Ornament (Made of Copper)

You can insert ten treasures (refer to page 138) into the mouth of this copper made Chinese unicorn and wrap five Emperors' old coins around the unicorn's body (refer to page 137). Then you pray for what you wish. Some feng shui masters use one Chinese unicorn, and the others use a pair. To start, you ought to start with one unicorn.

(Height: approximately 14 cm [5.5 inches])

A pair of Chinese unicorns exhibits maximum power
A Pair of Chinese Unicorns (Made of Copper)

A pair of male and female Chinese unicorns means yin and yang, and combined forces show the maximum power. A male holds a ball with his front foot and a female holds a child. When they are placed in the living room, the front door, the master bedroom, it will bring peace. Place the male on the right as you face it, and place the female on the left as you face it.

Pixiu
(Imaginary Animal)

Pixiu is an imaginary gentle animal, which has whiskers, a coiled tail and a horn. Its feature is charming, and it grants your every wish. Before the days of the Han period, it was called "a winged beast."

Its superior ability to accumulate wealth is well known, and if you are collecting henzai, it is said that there is no better feng shui animals.

Pixiu is placed indoors, and it is important to face its head toward the front door. If you do, it will bring in wealth to your house from all directions. Not only *henzai, but if you also want *syozai, it is important to put a Long Gui (a mystical dragon turtle) (refer to page 73) next to pixiu. By

placing both animals, the effect of increasing wealth will further increase. (*See next page.)

Generally, Pixiu is made of a pair of male and female, but if you are going to choose only one, choose a female. In a smaller size Pixiu, there are a male and female which share the same shape. If a male and female can be distinguished, the correct way to place them are that a male is placed on the left and a female is placed on the right looking from the front. There are many ways to increase Pixiu's power. For instance, if you insert the ancient ingot into its body, Pixiu gets the power of permanently collecting wealth without interruption. In addition, if you insert eight kinds of gems and jewels into Pixiu, it gets the power of collecting wealth from all the directions.

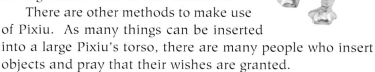

There are other methods to make use of Pixiu. As many things can be inserted into a large Pixiu's torso, there are many people who insert objects and pray that their wishes are granted.

Pixiu is a sacred beast which is very easy to handle, but its sole weakness is that it likes to sleep. Hang a bell called a "cow bell" around its neck, and ring the bell on and off to wake Pixiu up. The best place to place Pixiu is on the table or on the counter in the guest room, on the register, on the household shrine altar, on the television etc.

The more you cherish it, the more it responds to your wishes. Pixiu is indeed a daring animal, and you need to offer fresh water every day, and sometimes cleanse the air by burning incense such as sandalwood. When you devote it with you affection, it will work hard for you.

Pixiu is gentle but powerful, and it is a supreme feng shui item. It is often said that as you study feng shui, you eventually reach Pixiu.

*Henzai

Fluctuating income represented by financing business such as investment and banking, operating entertainment business such as mahjong, pachinko and a nightclub, and gambling.

*Syozai

Income earned by working diligently represented by promotion, successful business and sales transactions.

Wake up sleeping prosperity
Cow Bell

This is a bell to wake up sleepy Pixiu, and it needs to be hung around its neck. A red string is put through on the hole on the top of the bell, and you need to hang this around the neck of Pixiu. The sound of the bell has the effect of purifying maliciousness. It is a good idea to hang it in the front door or the bathroom door. The pattern on the cow bell indicates the best power to call in tranquility.

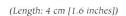

(Length: 4 cm [1.6 inches])

Long Gui
(Dragon Turtle)

Long Gui is a strange beast having a body of a turtle and a face of dragon. As its feature indicates, it has characteristics of both turtle and dragon. Long Gui belongs to the dragon families. It is a well known animal to increase prosperity. When you place it where business occurs in a company or a store, it will bring in riches continuously. That is why Long Gui is placed in a hotel in Las Vegas or in casino, and it is a feng shui item that is indispensable to people who are in business.

When you place Long Gui near gods and Buddhas, it is said that the effect of prosperity becomes immense. Long

Gui is used with Guan Yu and Fortune God (both gods of business).

In order to increase Long Gui's power, a crystal ball or ten treasures may be inserted into its body, or five Emperors' coins or six Emperors' coins may be wrapped around its body. Long Gui invites a noble man or restrains a white tiger which is a person who works against you, so you can enlarge positive connections with people. Furthermore, it prevents the evil spirits lingering on; by placing Long Gui near you. It will solve such problems as someting awful continuously happening or the feeling that something or someone is always stalking you. Because of these results, luck will turn in your favor.

In addition, if you place it on the desk where you work or study, it will assist your daily activities up. Long Gui is one of the most popular feng shui animals.

Yaazu Ornament

▌ *The strongest worrier among feng shui items*
Yaazu

There is a legend that a dragon bore nine babies—they are called the dragon's nine children. Among them, the seventh child, Yaazu, has been used for the pattern of amulets and weapons from the ancient times. Chinese emperors always kept Yaazu nearby.

Yaazu swallows the opponent's menace, and it kills and destroys bad energy coming from the opponent's menace. When it is kept in the house, it eats unfavorable energy and protects the home. Yaazu's energy is most strong, and its strength is enormous. All negative energies will be cleansed.

*Copper Made Yaazu Ornament
(Length 24.5 cm) [10 inches])*

The eyes of Yaazu are so sharp that they are considered god's eyes. When you stroke Yaazu's body with your left hand, it is said that your wishes would come true through god's insight. It is compatible with gold rutilated quartz, and if you place it near Yaazu, its efficacy is supposed to improve further. In order for Yaazu's power to work at its best, pour water and coarse salt in a cup, and place it near the mouth of Yaazu. Water needs to be changed daily while salt needs to be changed twice or so a month.

People who need to touch human bodies, i.e. nurses, masseurs etc., or those who consult people tend to receive negative energy from others. We recommend that you carry a portable Yaazu crystal engraving. When you go out, put it in your bag or a pocket, and occasionally take it out and hold it lightly with your left hand. It also has an effect of improving fortune, so it would be a good idea to carry it when you buy a lottery, take an examination, deal with business or face with a decisive moment in your life.

Portable Yaazu
(Width 5.5 cm) [2.2 inches]

Portable Yaazu
Crystal Engraving
(width approximately
2 cm) [0.8 inches]

Improves wealth and luck
Feng Shui Money Panther Ornament

A panther is a powerful animal just as a tiger and a lion, but it is not used to prevent evil spirits in feng shui. When you place this ornament in an office, a store or a house, not only it increases monetary luck, but also it releases people in these places from an atmosphere of menace.

(Length: approximately 28.5 cm [11 inches])

Fish that carries wealth and brings water energy
Arowana Ornament (Made of Copper)

In Chinese characters, a dragon and fish are written to describe arowana. Eyes and scales are the symbols of drag-

ons. Its shape is a weapon which was carried by military commanders. Arowana continues giving energy relating to the fortune of wealth.

It is said that if you want to improve your business fortune, place it on the desk or the place where you do your business, and the business will be a success.

If you want to improve economic fortune, place it in the direction of wealth in your company or a house.

In order to utilize the power of arowana to maximum, offer a glass of fresh water next to arowana's mouth every day.

Fortune comes!
Five Happiness Disk

A bat is also called a "lucky rat" in China, and it is considered as an auspicious animal and is well taken care of. A design that five bats are placed in a disk is a famous classic Chinese design. It means that all the good luck in life is

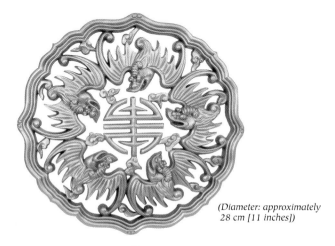

(Diameter: approximately 28 cm [11 inches])

gathered in its mouth. They are as follows:

- **Longevity:** living a long happy life.
- **Wealth:** have material comfort with a high social position.
- **Tranquility:** healthy body and peaceful mind.
- **Virtue:** performs good deeds and charity.
- **Happy ending:** no regrets at death and leaves this world peacefully.

However, some say that "happiness, stipend, longevity, joy and wealth" may be considered as five happinesses among the common people.

A bat invites happiness, and it demonstrates strong ability to prevent evil spirits as well. For instance, the evil spirit coming from supporting the ceiling will be erased by bats. The bat improves the health and luck.

Chinese Phoenix

The beautiful sacred bird was born with a peacock motif. It is said that the sacred bird that was born in imagination and appears to celebrate when a holy king comes in sight. The mythical Firebird Goddess has been respected as a bird of good omen to suggest prosperity and peace. A male is a large bird, and a female is a phoenix. It resembles a form of a chicken, but the whole body is richly variegated in color; you can see patterns in the Chinese characters of "virtue" in the neck, "justice" in the wing, "courtesy" in the back, "benevolence" in the chest, and "faith" in the abdomen.

A Chinese phoenix symbolizes inviting a nobleman, and when a Chinese phoenix is displayed in a woman's room, it is said that she will meet an ideal nobleman. The Chinese phoenix and the dragon tend to be used together.

Meet an ideal opposite sex
Chinese Phoenix Disk

It is a Chinese phoenix disk made of synthetic resins just as in the case of a "dragon disk" and a "dragon and Chinese phoenix disk." It is a recommended item for a woman who wants to meet an ideal man.

(Diameter: approximately 27.5 cm [10.8 inches])

Turtles

We are well acquainted with turtles among animals. In feng shui, we consider a turtle as an exemplary sacred beast, and we can often see turtle carvings in Taoist or Buddhist temples. Turtles are the symbols of longevity both in Japan and China, and putting a turtle in the house brings auspiciousness and fortune.

As the underside of a turtle is a concave carapace, it repels evil and makes the better feng shui environment. Although they are all sacred beasts, the expressions of dragons and Chinese unicorns give the impression of aspiration with dignity. Turtles, on the other hand, may be used as a symbol for stupidity as its movement is slow.

Nevertheless, there is a proverb in China that great wisdom looks foolish, which means that a truly extraordinary item appears seemingly foolish. This theory applies to Chinese martial arts such as Tai chi Chuan and Ba Gua. Turtles do not hold down evil with force, but they utilize and take in the power of evil. By doing so, it neutralizes evil and throws it into auspiciousness. Since feng shu ieffect is very low key, it best applies to remove evil from homes where there are an adult, a small child and sick person at home.

A feng shui turtle may be placed near an older person or a sick person's bedside, so the turtle will inhale evil and disgorge an auspicious aura.

The turtle's actions are slow, but they are patient and go forward in orderly manner. So they represent indomitable spirit, and because of that, it is used to improve business fortune. They are frequently used for the promotion of business, expanding of the business market and becoming independent owner of business. Because ceramic is broken easily, a turtle made of metal is used. The most effective metal is copper or brass. Regarding the location to place a metal turtle, the west or northern west which are the places for gold of the five elements of traditional Chinese philosophy.

When a turtle decorates a family Buddhist altar, it improves the family's finance. It needs to be placed on the left of the altar in the front. The preferable turtle is made of precious stone, but a copper turtle is acceptable. It is best to avoid a gold turtle because, needless to say, Buddha is the leading character of the altar.

As a turtle is auspicious and is effective against any evil, it is widely used. Because of gentle effectiveness, there are specific ways to use a turtle. For instance, you do not know about your next door neighbor, but you have a hunch that the neighbor is decorating their house with a strong "energy" item which is placed toward the direction of your house, or you have a hunch that the "energy" item is flowing bad "energy" to your house. Then you need to use a turtle made of copper to avoid evil spirit. The method is to place one or a few turtles between your house and the neighbor's house. The turtle does not emit evil spirits, but it captures the other's evil spirit but changes it into positive spirit.

Furthermore, if having only a turtle figure does not give enough feng shui power, old copper money may be used with a turtle as it will increase power. (Pp. 196) In this case, place a copper turtle in the middle of a small plate, and put yin and yang eight old coins.

Neutralize and erase evil spirit!
A Copper Turtle Ornament

   A turtle is a sign of longevity in Japan, but as a feng shui item, it brushes off maliciousness.   As the shell of a turtle draws an arc just like a convex mirror, it will hit back negative energy in the room. The negative spirit arises between two tall buildings. When this evil spirit is seen from a balcony or a window, place a pair of turtles next to them; it will change the negative to positive energy.   It is an indispensable item for an attic.   A slanted ceiling and beam are not favorably regarded in feng shui.   If you live in the attic, many arguments or disagreements happen to come about and you may not be able to live comfortably.   So, use a turtle to arrange the surroundings.

Win over your rival and increase your fortune
Cobra (Made of Copper)

In feng shui, in order to bring in good energy from outside, we place a figure something like a baseball mitt near the front door or windows. The bulge of a cobra's collar acts the same way as a baseball mitt. A cobra symbolizes wealth and excellent luck; furthermore, it will put pressure on people you do not want to associate with, those who have thirst for blood or your business enemy. It will attack them with strong toxin, and they will be wiped out.

There has been a long economic slump, and time has been hard. There is only one feng shui figure having aggressiveness against the outside as well as defense capability while it captures the fortune of wealth, and that is a cobra. Ordinarily, the cobra has eight Ba Gua old coins both collars as if it was a family crest, and it brings in more power. (See P. 135) The best place to place the cobra is near the front door, and it is important to face it to outside.

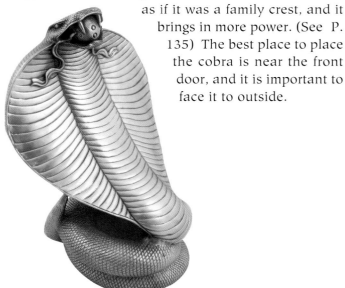

Peck at negative energy
Chicken (Made of Copper)

When there are fire escape ladders outside the building across from your place, it reminds of a centipede which springs forth negative energy. It is regarded as bad feng shui. When this situation happens, place a chicken figure made of copper over the window facing the ladders. A chicken eats insects, and it pecks at negative energy sprang by the centipede.

If family members do not get along and you feel negative energy, it would be a good idea to place it in the living room or the bed room. It will peck at grumpiness or infidelity and solve the core of the problem.

(Height: about 7 cm [2.8 inches])

Gathering up riches
Three Legged Copper Toad

The characteristic of this toad is three legs. It is said that the toad collects all the wealth found in the front, left, and right of itself. It is considered as a professional money collecting toad (ornament), and it is a very popular item.

Having collected a lot of money, the toad places itself on the money and even takes money in its mouth. It appears as if the toad wants to save up even more money. He looks like a dependable financial official. It is certainly a feng shui item to increase wealth. The three legged toad will boost possessions remarkably, and it is especially effective for the growth of business. It is usually placed at the front door of an office or a store.

In order for the toad to be very active, you turn its face toward the front door where business takes place in the start of a business day. Likewise, you should shift the face to the room at the end of a business day, and it is also important to strokes its head then. Gradually, its face becomes luminous and demonstrates its strength. Then you will become so attached to it, and you can never be apart from it.

When you keep the toad in the front door or your room in your house, do the same thing. When you leave for work, move the face toward outside. When you come home, turn the face inside and show your gratitude.

It is said that the toad has a master. He is a legendary immortal mountain wizard known as Ryukaisen; however, his real name is Ryoukaisou.

It is said that if you say, "Calling Master Rooukai", the toad will throw all the treasure he has accumulated.

In addition to the toad ornament, there is another ornament: "Great king three legged toad."

You do not use this toad when you want only the material wealth. Seeing far into the future, you want to attain transcending power, and that is when you display this toad. When displayed together with the tree legged toad, the power will further increase.

CHAPTER 4

Attain your desire
with the power of
crystal and stones

IN FUNG SHUI, THERE ARE MANY WAYS
TO UTILIZE THE POWER OF NATURAL
STONES SO THAT YOU ATTAIN YOUR DE-
SIRE. THIS CHAPTER WILL SHOW YOU
HOW YOU WILL EXTRACT THE POWER
OF STONES AT THEIR MAXIMUM AND
ACTIVATE THEIR POWER.

Your fortune will increase tremendously
Phantom Pyramid Quartz
(Dragon Vein Crystal)

The process of crystal has been formulated over many thousands of years similar to the rings of a tree, and it is called "Dragon vein crystal." The crystal is known throughout the world to promote better fortune on a daily basis. It is regarded as crystal to improve fortune, and in Chinese cultural sphere, it is especially regarded as valuable. It will support your fortune including business, personal relationships, wealth and such. Miraculously, the mountain shaped crystal goes through with infinite variety of changes in vividness and hue. It is said that it adjusts the energy balance between the crystal and its owner.

Generally, crystal is worn as a pendant, but a large hexagonal prism is placed in the house or office as a treasure to increase fortune. It is a lifelong treasure, and it is indeed the case with this crystal that dominates fortune. It is passed down from a grandfather to a father to a child, and it is definitely a treasure.

Gather wealth and activate it!
Amethyst Dome

This is a traditional feng shui method to call in fortune, and it is an essential item to activate your luck. Amethyst is a known stone to increase fortune, and it is cut right in the middle. Place it in the front door or exit; then it will call the fortune flowing outside in. So, generally it is placed in the front of the front door or exit. It may be a good idea to place it near a safe or a cash register. If you place it behind the desk at workplace, your brain will be activated, and the ability to concentrate and your vitality will increase. Yu can insert an appropriate crystal ball in the dome to make your wishes come true. Which direction or what type of a dome you would place will vary the result of fortune, and it is one of a charm,

Turn out a power spot
Treasure Agate

Agate in the rough is cut in half. An upper lid will catch wealth and various luck, and the captured luck will be put inside the hollow of the tray. There are many crystals. Simply by placing a treasure agate, positive energy will be called in and a strong power spot will be turned out. Place it facing the entrance of the front door or the direction of wealth in the room. Place it throughout the house as well as the center of the house. If you find the stairs as you open the front door, place treasure agate when you reach the top of the stairs. If a power stone pertaining to your objective is placed in the hole of the tray, it will increase the power to grant your wish. There are many colors, and it heals your mind just by watching.

Makes barrier!
Black Crystal (Morion)

Black crystal is used with a prayer or the purification of all the negative energies flowing on the ground. If there are a shrine, a temple, a funeral home, a hospital in your surroundings, make a barrier by placing a black crystal.

If there is a bridge facing your company or store directly, your wealth will deteriorate. In order to block the negative energy, place a black crystal to both ends of the front door and the exit to create a barrier.

If the kitchen is situated in the center of a house, use a black crystal. It is bad luck to have the trace of fire in the middle of the house; apart from bad luck, it is not a good idea from the point of disaster prevention. By putting a black crystal near a fire, it will change to good luck.

Purification of the land and a building
A Set of Crystal Balls for Purification

In feng shui it is usual to bury crystal balls under the ground when a house or a building is built. To start with, bury four crystal balls in four corners and bury a little bit larger crystal in the middle of the ground. By doing so, the site will be purified, and you will receive a lot of power from the ground. You would actually feel the people get luckier who live there. The same applies for a store and workplace. We recommend that you will bury crystal before you build a building.

If it is difficult to bury crystal, hang a crystal ball from a ceiling or a wall.

(Diameter: 40 mm [16 inches] x 1 crystal ball)
(Diameter: 28mm [11 inches] x 4 crystal balls)

Purification of the bathroom (toilet)
A Crystal Ball Inserted in a Purple Bag

A bathroom (toilet) tends to become filthy, and negative energy tends to congregate there. In order to purify the negative energy of the room, many techniques have been tried. Among these, it is known that the easiest but most effective method is to insert a crystal ball in a purple net bag and hang on the wall. Keep the bathroom (toilet) clean and try this method.

If you are going to build a bathroom (toilet), there is an effective method to bury a lot of crystal pebbles under the floor of the bathroom (toilet.) There are other methods to place hexagonal prisms on four corners of the bathroom (toilet): place salt under the flushing tank, place crystal ball in the tank etc. We have a negative image of the bathroom (toilet) and the kitchen having unpleasant odor. In order to correct it, there are methods to hang an energy stabilizer or multifaceted crystal ball as well.

Purification specialist
Crystal Pebbles

These is an ideal items to purify a place, and it applies to any places. It prevents the bad influences caused by negative energy. It is specially recommended to put the pebbles in front of the front door or the place where water is used. It is also said that placing them in a pillow will give you a good night's sleep. It has been done from the past to bury or sprinkle pebbles in the ground prior to the construction of a building. (A standard amount is 1 kg [2.2 pounds] per 1 tsubo [approximately 3.3m²]) Power stones or accessories may be placed on top of pebbles to purity, or pebbles may be inserted into the dirt of a flowerpot to increase the power held by plants.

Sleep well and peaceful mind
Amethyst Pebbles

Where people encounter and create something, amethyst pebbles exhibit great power. If you are going to build an office, a study, a research laboratory and such, we recommend placing amethyst pebbles under the floor. For the space you are currently using as an office or a study, place them on the desk; your abilities to concentrate will increase. Amethyst heals emotions, so if you put pebbles in the pillow or on a floor cushion, your mind would become calm, and you will be able to spend a peaceful and quiet time.

| *Increase women's charm*
Rose Quartz Pebbles

It is said that rose quartz will increase women's charms and have successful relationship. Just displaying it in the room, it will miraculously calm down your mind and you will smile. Because of that, personal relationships will become better, and you will have more chances to meet new people. It is recommended for people whose occupations depend on public favor, who want to expand personal connections and for men as well. If you place them on the counter top in the bathroom or in front of the make-up mirror, you would become more beautiful.

Support wealth
Gold Rutilated Quartz Pebbles

A gold rutilated quartz is a well known power stone to increase wealth greatly. Gold rutilated quartz pebbles assist various feng shui items. Put them into Pixiu or into a dragon jar, or put them near the items relating money, the effort of gathering wealth will increase. Putting it into the safe with an ingot is another effective way.

Heal with light
Crystal Healing Lamp

This is a dimly lit incandescent lamp buried inside natural crystal. It is an exclusive lamp for people living in contemporary time to rest. Because the soft color is lit from the inside natural crystal, it makes you truly feel rested with calming energy. The natural crystal used here is not translucent. It has absorbed a plenty of the earth's

energy and has been growing for thousands of years. Using the industry terms, the natural crystal here are "only those that have many years of experience".

Crystal has been known to invite luck throughout the world, and yet research is being conducted whether crystal will bring more luck when a certain stimuli are given to crystal.

Purification and increasing power
Crystal Clusters

A quantity of crystal gathered and produced in the crystal mine is called a cluster. Adding to its beauty, it shows synergistic effect in clusters as crystal energy compounds, and it is popular as it is especially good at purifying environment. Furthermore, crystal balls or a various power stones are placed on top of the clusters, it increases fortune. When you put your accessories, such as bracelets, rings, necklaces etc., among clusters, it naturally purifies negative and suspicious energy which might have been compressed in them.

Elegant and Power up!
Plating Crystal Clusters (Golden Clusters)

When crystal clusters are gold plated with a special technique, we call them golden clusters. This objet d'art which shines golden is elegant and looks as if each crystal is showing off its beauty. It has energy to increase wealth. Potential capacities and result to increase fortune is the same as crystal clusters. Putting crystal clusters with natural color and golden color side by side, purifies accessories or power stones. As compatibility with different power stones becomes visible, I recommend that you study compatibility with purification on your own.

Calm your nerves!
Healing-Cut-Crystal

What is introduced here is a special crystal on which a special healing polish was applied. We live in a stressful modern competitive lifestyle; and yet, no one can avoid living differently. When you feel very stressed, softly take a healing-cut-crystal in your hand. It will surely calm you down.

- ◆ Stressful
- ◆ Irritable
- ◆ Feel gloomy
- ◆ Get tense
- ◆ Your heart flatters
- ◆ Break into a cold sweat
- ◆ Can't fall asleep
- ◆ Have a nightmare
- ◆ Have a dream that isn't granted
- ◆ Want to work that you can concentrate
- ◆ Feels on edge in front of people
- ◆ Wants to heighten the ability to concentrate instantly
- ◆ Successful examinations and business

You ought to try to find a suitable healing-cut-crystal for you. It will become your lifetime partner and comfort you.

If Healing-cut-crystal is a gift for your important person, your thoughtfulness would be appreciated.

The natural crystal used for healing-cut-crystal is not always transparent just as in the case of a crystal lamp. It has absorbed a plenty of the earth's energy and has been growing for thousands of years. Using the industry terms, the natural crystal are "only those that have many years of experience". It has a power of healing; when you hold softly, it will loosen your tension. As the natural shape is to be utilized, the surface is softly polished. It feels cool and give you good feeling, and you would actually feel the effect of calming.

The healing-cut-crystal made by the crystal in which water and air were shut out in the crystal for thousands of years emits especially powerful energy.

Amplify energy!
Crystal Spinner Which Turns Crystal around from the Ceiling

Place a crystal ball on a spiral crystal spinner made of brass, which is a revolving pedestal to hold a crystal ball, hang it from the ceiling as shown in the picture. Powered by natural air flow, the crystal ball starts to swing and revolve repeatedly. As the crystal spinner takes a role of a spring, a small amount of energy is amplified and reaches the crystal ball. While the crystal ball placed on the crystal spinner repeats swinging and rotation, it scatters glittering crystal energy as if it were snow shower made of cut paper. It is even more effective if it is an electric rotating machine.

Expands energy
Moving Display for a Crystal Ball

A rotating style display case often seen in a jewelry shop or boutique is an appropriate tool to vibrate a crystal ball and spray energy.

Improve the energy of power stones

Rotating Display Case that Illuminates Crystal

There has been a lot of research done from the ancient time to further heighten the energy possessed by crystal or power stone. What needs to be specially mentioned is a method to put light on crystal or power stone. If you use a display case which has a built in LED illuminant, it becomes possible to illuminate from below with a ray of light. It actually becomes a crystal energy studded room. The LED is able to scatter the energy of crystal and power stone. Further research is being conducted. You can purchase this product in professional fortune stores.

A work of art created by nature
Dripstone

Milk stone has been used in China to warm up a body. As there is a proverb saying that milk stone slides off stone, it disperses just like frost and snow. It has been made by the eternal solid earth and water just as the same as crystal. Water containing dripping calcium has made a stone which looks like icicles. The falling drops of water have hit the stone, scattered and made such shapes as flowers, coral, animals etc. It is highly valued as it has immense effect on the realization of a great ambition, improving fortune, and peace and prosperity in the household.

CHAPTER 5

☯

Dispose negative energy and stabilize energy

YOU NEED TO ELIMINATE EVIL ENERGY AT
FIRST IN ORDER TO PUT YOUR FUNG SHUI
ENVIRONMENT IN ORDER. THIS CHAPTER
WILL INTRODUCE YOU APPROPRIATE
ITEMS TO ELIMINATE EVIL ENERGY.

Amulet and improvement of fortune
Natural Crystal Ba Gua Yin and Yang Pendant

A natural crystal Ba Gua pendant is very popular as a feng shui amulet. It gives crystal power to increase the fortune of wealth, love, jobs etc. as well as guide you as you wish in life, Ba Gua which keeps all of your dislikes at a distance, and Yin and Yang power which draws out not yet found your potential capacities and further activate your fortune. By putting this on, it is said that you will be happier.

A chain can be attached, and you might like to wear as a pendant. If worn by a young woman, it will protect her from a sexual molester or a stalker.

When you place them on the four corners of your car, they protect you from a car accident. It also increases your finances and winning of games as well as stabilizing emotion. As you can see, it is an all-purpose feng shui item.

(Width: approximately 2.5cm [1 inch])

It keeps the enemy off
Pure Silver Yin and Yang Pendant with Silver Mirror

This is a pure silver yin and yang pendant with the silver mirror that will protect you from all bad energy. There is a crystal mirror with diamond cuts in the center of the pendant. The crystal which has diamond cuts in the center is placed on top of the 24 gold plate. Since diamond cut crystal has diffusing power, you can keep clear of what you do not like as you keep the pendant on you. It is appropriate to wear to avert traffic accidents, encountering a molester or a stalker away from you. It is recommended for those who want to be fashionable with feng shui effect.

Exterminate evil aura
Spiritual Peach Tree Wood Sword

In ancient China, peach trees were regarded as a sort of cosmic trees, and even today, it is considered as a sort of sacred trees. It is said that when the heavenly gods descend to the earth filled with troubles, they wash themselves with hot water containing a piece of peach tree bark without fail. Peach trees have dual functions—cleansing and removing evil spirits. This spiritual peach tree wood sword is a sacred sword, and it removes the unseen evil spirits. If you feel negative energy near your house or your house is dark and feel the presence of evil spirit, display a spiritual peach tree wood sword in the northeastern (unlucky) direction or in the unlucky quarter (southwest.) If the problems are related to your ancestors, display near your family altar. If you display it near the household Shinto shrine in your house, it keeps comfortable airspace for gods.

(Length: approximately 28 cm [11 inches])

Absorb negative energy
Natural Filter: Gourd

Natural gourds are feng shui air cleaners which absorb bad energy. Crystal pebbles and such are placed in a gourd. (Refer to page 95) Putting it in the open space around you, it will absorb the bad energy that surrounds you on a daily basis, and it will protect you.

If a family member is not well, hang it on the exit and/or entrance of his or her room. To be specific, it will absorb illness when you place a gourd's mouth in the direction of the head of a patient, and the patient will recover from illness quickly.

(Length: approximately 50 cm [19.6 inches])

You can also expect the effect of a charm against evil spirits as a gourd absorbs the evil souls of ghosts and demons. A gourd also absorbs the menace of demons coming from a building. When a beam is shown on the ceiling, it generates evil spirits and disturbs the harmony in space. In this case, prepare two gourds and two copper bells, and hang from the beam. The sound of bells weakens the evil spirits and cleanses them. However, do not forget to keep the gourd's mouth open as it can capture the evil spirits.

Solves disagreeable problems!
(The final method to improve your fortune)
Feng Shui Sword and Ginger

Many unforeseen worries, problems, calamities suddenly occur in life. Before you become distressed thinking what to do or there is nothing you can do, we recommend that you practice the methods to improve your luck. It has been practiced since the ancient time, and an amazing positive effect has been shown.

1. Prepare feng shui swords (a Shang Fang Bao or a seven star sword), ginger and a dishcloth.

2. Picture a problem you want to solve in your mind. While hoping the problem to be solved, rub a feng shui sword with the dishcloth. One word of caution is that an unreasonable wish or that with malicious and hostile intent is not going to receive any effect.

3. When you rub the sword until you feel satisfied, stab ginger with the feng shui sword and make sure that ginger juice oozes out. If it is not oozing out, the effect will be weaker.

4. Place it in the front door where it isn't in the way of coming and going. If it cannot be placed there, there is no problem to place it in the kitchen or in the room.

*Following the procedures 1 through 4, change the stabbing position every day. Repeat this until the problem is solved. You can do as many times as you like per day. It is important, however, to make sure juice oozes out from ginger every time you stab it. When the ginger no longer oozes juice out, you need a new one. The used ginger must be placed in a bag with sea salt, and you need to purify it and dispose it.

Put into practice!

Use a treasure inviting sword and ginger to tackle visible events.

◆ Matrimonial quarrel
◆ Your child/children are bullied
◆ Your neighbors are spiteful.
◆ Someone is always picking a fight with you.
◆ Sexual harassment by your boss
◆ The worst daughter-in-law and mother-in-laws problem
◆ There is a person hard to deal with in your office or business connection
◆ You get many troublesome sales calls or direct marketing calls

Use a seven star sward and ginger to tackle invisible events,
- Being pursued by a stalker or someone you do not know
- Tends to be possessed by supernatural things
- Receives a lot of annoying email
- Feels something supernatural when you get into the room
- Receive silent phone calls
- Have a nightmare
- Tendency to catch a cold
- Tendency to get hurt physically

Destroy negative spirits and energy!
Seven Star Sword Made of Copper

It is called a treasure or a legal sword, and it is a weapon to destroy invisible negative spirits and energy. If you use a peach wooden sword with a seven star sword at the same time, the ability to purify evil spirit will strengthen to the fullest. Even the bad influence caused by your star sign or your presently stagnating fortune will terminate and will turn your fortune better.

Purify evil spirit
A Latticed Stick

This is a stick which shuts out evil thought or evil energy. You hang on the upper portion of the entrance and the exit where there is possibility of trespassing. It is a reliable item to protect you from evil energy or danger.

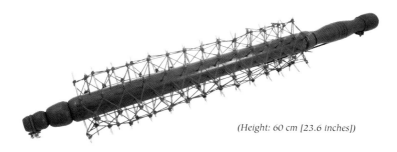

(Height: 60 cm [23.6 inches])

Prevent an intrusion of evil
A Latticed Ball

This is a latticed ball on which ten or more protruding nails shaped like radial rays are twined round with red strings. It is a well known feng shui item—the frightening form will prick powerful evil energy through nails. If you hang this in the front door or exit, an evil spirit will not be able to come in.

(Length: approximately 40 cm [16 inches])
(The diameter of ball: approximately 7cm [2.7 cm])

Prevent the intrusion of negative energy
Lion Yin and Yang Ba Gua Plain Mirror

Simply by hanging these items in the room needing protection, evil energy will change for the better by the power of lion, Ba Gua yin and yang, stone monument and an amulet. It is an indispensable item for a corner. You need to place it on the corner of the wall you are facing, the entrance and exit where you can see a fire hydrant or an elevator, and you must shut out the evil energy. If there are places near your house where evil energy tends to gather, i.e. at a cemetery, a large hospital, a Shinto shrine without the chief priest present, and a deserted house, the mirror should be installed facing toward the direction.

(Large: Length 26 cm [10 inches] and width 19 cm [7.5 inches])
(Small: Length 16 cm [6 inches] and width 9 cm [3.5 inches])

The divine stone which catches all the evil energy
A Stone Monument

Evil spirits and bad energy moves straight ahead. There is a fear that a building located at the end of a T junction or a building facing a T-junction might catch evil energy directly and will deteriorate. The stone monument has evil spirits thrown to the monument and draws away negative energy. If a building is located at the same height as a traffic high-way, place the monument facing the evil energy. Usually "Mount Taishan" is written on the monument, but to strengthen the protective power, there are those which have the inscriptions of Ba Gua, a lion's face or a tiger's face, and a beetle. They are often found in Okinawa, Taiwan, Singapore and such.

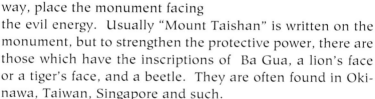

Cleanse wickedness and invite fortune! "The ultimate secret"
Xingren Water

Xingren water is a symbolic fung sui item that brings luck. You place six Emperor coins and a dragon silver (silver coin) in the salt which had sank into salty water. It is effective even if only the six Emperors' coins are placed; however, when a silver coin called a dragon coin is used, the strong power that a dragon has is added, and unthinkable big fortune may be expected. In addition, when Xingren water and various feng shui items are used together, it will activate even further.

There were many old coins in ancient China, and their feng shui effects vary, but it doesn't mean that any old coins will work. Among the ten Emperors who reigned during Qing Dynasty (1644-1912) , the most powerful six Emperors issued copper coins, and that is called the six Emperors' copper coins. They are as follows: Shun Ye coin, Kang Xi coin, Yong Zheng coin, Gan long coin, Jia Qing coin and Dao Guang coin

The prices of both six Emperors' old coins and dragon silver have gone up, and it has become difficult to obtain genuine articles. Because of that, imitation coins are rampant. (These imitations are made very elaborately.) Unless it is a genuine feng shui article, a result cannot be expected.

Needless to say, if Xingren water is used with various feng shui items, its effect can be further strengthen.

☯

Xingren Water does the following:
◆ Solves misfortune, accidents, bad influence.
◆ Avoids verbal problems and troubles caused by human relationships
◆ Invites wealth
◆ Restrains negative actions caused by Wuhuangsha, Dashajie of "fortune – telling"

*Six emperor coins and
a dragon silver coin
sank into salty water*

After several weeks

Improves purifying effect
Cooper Gourd Incense Burner

Incense is burned in feng shui to purify a place. It is a feng shui item that cleanses bad energy and purifies energy flowing in its space. A gourd works to collect negative energy, so a burner shaped like a gourd increases the degree of purification and speed up the process. In addition, because it has an effect of absorbing a demon and a devil, if it is displayed at your bedside, it is said to absorb negative energy causing illness.

(Large: Approximate height 17 cm [6.7 inches])
(Medium: Approximate height 12 cm [4.7 inches])
(Small: Approximate height 9.5 cm [3.7 inches])

Purifies everything
Sandalwood Incense

This is an exclusive incense to cleanse a place. In order to purify all feng shui items, it is best to burn incense every day. There is a healing effect which has been talked about from ancient time.

(Diameter: approximately 4 cm [1.6 inches])

Works as a purifier for a space
Ceramics Ba Gua Incense Burner

This is an incense burner made of ceramics. Yin Yang Ba Gua is chiseled. It purifies and stabilizes the area. When crystal pebbles are put in the burner, it works as a purifier for the space. It may be used as a container for a bracelet or accessories in order for them to be purified.

Purifies and draws happiness towards you
Copper Feng Shui Incense Burner

This is an elaborately designed powerful incense burner with a serious thought of feng shui in mind. Nine dragons are carved in the burner including on its lid. Furthermore, on three legs supporting the burner, a lion with strong ability to draw away evil spirits is engraved. A tiger eye ball which increases wealth is installed on top of the lid. The two dragons placed next to the tiger eye ball function to further increase the power of tiger eyes.

By burning incense in the burner, it purifies negative energy, and the dragon which symbolizes wealth and happiness increases your fortune for wealth, business, health, love and all others. Thus, it arranges the space that you can live happily.

If you place it in the entrance or in the living room, it may be used as an interior object.

Wipe out all the negative energy
Evil Removing Incense

You need a feng shui item to purify a house or a room in which you feel hindrance (feeling chills.) This product is the exclusive incense to remove all the obstacles. For instance, you are moving to a previously occupied house, a rental apartment, an office etc. If the previous tenant's energy remains there, there is a chance of being influenced negatively. Therefore, it is necessary to purify the place by burning incense upon moving to the new place. In addition, if you feel bad energy while living there, you will have a good effect if you burn incense.

There may be people who feel unwell after going to such places as a funeral home, a hospital, and a temple or they feel rundown after taking a trip, taking care of sick people and such because they may have much negative energy surrounding those places. In such instances, they must be bathed with the smoke of incense and purify negative energy.

Where there is a shrine, a Buddhist temple (cemetery), a funeral home, a hospital, etc. near your house or office, place a lion Ba Gua flat mirror, a flat calming mirror (see page 27) and a seven star sward (p. 109) facing the house or the office. After that, burn evil-removing incense.

CHAPTER 6

☯

Luck will change just by carrying or affixing these items!

THERE ARE MANY FUNG SHUI ITEMS THAT WILL IMPROVE YOUR FORTUNE JUST BY CARRYING THEM, OR HANGING OR AFFIXING THEM IN A ROOM OR AN OFFICE. THIS CHAPTER WILL INTRO-DUCE THOSE FUNG SHUI ITEMS THAT YOU CAN TRY WITH EASE.

| *For improving wealth, there is nothing better!*
| Feng Shui Fortune Wallet

This is a wallet which satisfies all the feng shui requirements to improve wealth according to the feng shui theory.

1) A designed button to improve wealth

Four Chinese auspicious letters are written on the button. It means to invite wealth and get richer.

2) Wealth god gold card

A traditional wealth god is especially popular with overseas Chinese. It brings everyone wealth and gratification including the children who are the symbol of luck.

3) Dragon design
As two dragons are facing each other, they exchange their energy and create new energy.

4) Secret pocket
Insert a lottery, an admission ticket for an examination, and your wishes in a hidden pocket in the wallet.

5) A design of two Chinese phoenixes facing each other
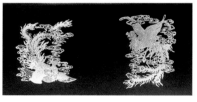
Drawn in the hidden pocket of the wallet, it resonates with the energy of two dragons facing each other, and it further helps to grow wealth.

6) A dragon ball with tiger eye stone

Two dragons facing each other spring forth a great amount of energy in the center. There in the middle of the center, a dragon eye (using tiger eye stone) is inserted. The tiger eye stone increases wealth.

7) Measurement design for money
It is a good measurement for money because an auspicious measurement (length) was applied.

gold color: It has a power to invite luck concerning money and set the luck in motion.

black color: It has a power to stabilizes luck concerning money.

Protect from evil things
Ba Gua Eyeball Agate

An eyeball agate protects you from every kind of danger because it increases your own defense mechanism. It has been treated with care as a stone to protect from evil and negative energy. Its wide open eyes see through the real nature of matters, and it even stops the attacks one gets from the surroundings. When you feel that jealousy, resentment, and hatred are surrounding you, you need to wear Ba Gua eyeball agate. In China, if one is possessed, there is a method to call an evil spirit by rubbing a body of the person with this stone and absorb the evil spirit.

Invites good luck
Eight White Stones

Eight white stones will radiate together, and they are auspicious for wealth, business, human relations, and childbirth. They are lucky items. For some reason or other, if you feel your luck is not good, decorate your front and back door with eight white stones. As eight white stones contain a lot of good energy, evil spirits and decaying energy will be solved. You should carry them at all times when a human relationship is not working out or your health is not well.

Beam on the ceiling
Crystal Suppression Hanging
(Ya Sha Shui Jing Shi Wo Shuai)

A beam warps the flow of energy, and it gives a sense of oppression to people live under the beam. The best way is to move from under the beam, but if it is difficult, hang a crystal suppression hanging to both sides of the beam and draw bad energy out.

The upper portion of the crystal suppression hanging is a crystal ball where natural crystal was cut multilaterally. It softens the bad energy directly coming from the beam by the diffusion of light and draws it away. The bottom figure symbolizes yin and yang. This figure brings harmony to all natural life, and the new energy flow may be formed.

Almighty amulet!
Universal Light Fixing Hanging
(Qian Kun Zha Bao Tu)

This is an almighty item that works for you so that everything comes true. It removes evils, arranges home life, and invites peace at home. When light is too bright, the positive side becomes too

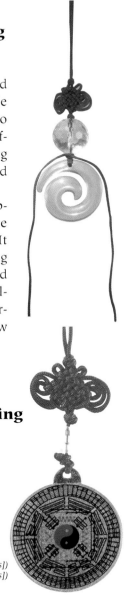

(Diameter: approximately 3cm [1.1 inches])
(Length: approximately 20~40 cm [7.9~15.8 inches])

strong, so irritation, arguments and disharmonious relation-ships occur. When light is too dark, on the other hand, the negative side becomes too strong, so bad energy, negative thoughts, illness etc. are drawn. If there is the disorder of light within the room, this item will correct the needed balance.

Improves your fortune!
Dragon Pendant

Crystal has a characteristic of water, and it controls en-ergy balance that exists on the earth. Wearing it, it will ab-sorb your negative energy and increase positive energy. So, it will get rid of var-ious stress and pull out your potential capacities.

A dragon is said to symbolize energy which runs through the ground and has immeasurable power, and the dragon becomes active by the power of water. The dragon wrapped around a crystal ball or en-graved in crystal gained the power of water. This dragon pendant will give you health, courage, and liveliness; it will turn around your fortune into better.

Make dragon power your ally!
Brass Dragon Door Handle

Simply by switching to a brass dragon door handle, dragon power will become your friend. When you use the door handle, dragon energy will move in a lively way and good energy will increase.

(Length: approximately 28.5 cm [11 inches])

Improve the luck of business and trade
Large Silk Fan with Two Dragons Facing

Golden dragons facing each other are drawn on a large silk fan. The dragons will carry fortune on them and move toward the heaven. It especially improves the luck of business and trade, so it is recommended to display as an interior ornament in the office or the store.

(Width: 152.4 cm [60 inches])

Seal to avoid evil spirits
Ba Gua Seal

This is a seal to keep away all of what you dislike; it drives off evil spirits. It is very convenient to have this around as the sticker will make it possible to utilize the power of the Ba Gua wherever you may be. It is highly recommended for safe driving and blocking off evil spirits.

(Width of seal: approximately 8.5 cm [3.3 inches])

God of learning and successful carrier
Card Symbolizing the God of Learning

Through the teaching of Confucius, Confucius is the god of learning, and Chu Hsi is respected as the god of examination and successful carrier. Both gods are drawn in gold plated cards, and they are amulets for the better learning and carrier.

As a matter of fact, the foundation of learning must have truth; you do not gain anything just to learn subjects by rote or just to think about them in your mind but do not apply them. When you keep cards of god of learning and success with you, you acquire true knowledge. You will be able to score higher than anticipated while taking examinations. Likewise, your boss is going to like you and pay positive attention to you, which in return, will help you getting promotion on your job.

(Height: approximately 8 cm [3 inches])

Finishing Touches for Purification of Evil Spirits
Mayokettchi (Wall Hanging)

Hizyashishigashira, nicknamed as Mayokettchi, is hung in a house, a shop, an office and such. It is a feng shui item to protect from evil spirits, and you hang them after the fang shui space is properly arranged. When you hang them at the front door, the northeastern direction (unlucky), and southwest (the unlucky) evil spirits cannot get in, and good feng shui environment may be maintained.

If you have any other directions or places that you are concerned about, it is a good idea to hang Mayokettchi. Evil spirits will be shut out, and it keeps good feng shui environment. It can be used anywhere including your workplace or home. Generally we change a hanging once a year if it is a small sized one.

(Left: Width between small horns: approximately 7.8 cm [3 inches])
(Large: Width between large horns: approximately 30 cm [11.5 inches])

Wall hanging for wealth and luck
Bamboo Hanging with Red Tassel

A bamboo is a symbol of wealth. It invites wealth and luck. This is a traditional hanging with a red tassel. As you invite wealth, you become wealthy. That is the reason why there is a pair of hangings, one for inviting wealth and another for getting richer. The pair symbolizes yin and yang; it brings energy and gives power to produce new things. It would be a good idea to hang a pair in the living room, the front door and near the cash register in the store.

Put it at your eye level
Fortune God

This god is well known for possessing strong power to increase your wealth and summon good fortune. Simply by hanging the panel where the fortune god is drawn, your fortune will improve miraculously. In order to improve your fortune, however, the location has to be carefully studied, and it has to be at your eye level.

(Height: 23 cm [9 inches], Width: 14cm [5.5 inches])

Height
- ◆ At home, it has to be at the eye level with a major wage earner, the head of the family.
- ◆ Put a feng shui ruler on the floor, and the eyes of the god will

be leveled where the following items are shown: 1. win in a lottery, 2. become rich, 3. prosperity, 4. wealth and virtue, and 5. win a gamble

Location

A. According to the decision of a feng shui master, the sign of wealth will be decided.

B. A place where most people will ordinarily enter so that they can get to the above A, which is ordinarily the front door

There are many cases to hang both A and B above if you desire to have stronger results. If the panel is too conspicuous or the design is not to your liking, you can hide it with a curtain, a calendar or a poster. The effect of the god will produce will not change.

A well known compatible feng shui item with the fortune god is a dragon turtle that also increases wealth. It is an inseparable item from the fortune or business gods. By placing a dragon turtle ornament near the panel, the power to increase wealth will improve due to the synergistic effect. Put them together to increase your money and business. You might like to carry a gold plated card with the picture of fortune god in your wallet.

CHAPTER 7

☯

More good fortune comes when combined with other items

THERE ARE FENG SHUI ITEMS THAT
INCREASE POWER WHEN COMBINED
WITH OTHER ITEMS. IN THIS CHAPTER,
THOSE ITEMS THAT WILL INCREASE
FENG SHUI EFFECT TO THE MAXIMUM
WILL BE INTRODUCED.

Feng Shui items
which use old coins

In feng shui, copper old coins belong to gold element in the five elements of traditional Chinese philosophy: wood, fire, earth, metal and water. It is a popular and effective feng shui item to destroy evil energy. It also keeps harmony at home and workplace, prospers your fortune, and increases good energy as well as never cuts off money supplies.

Not only an indispensable lucky item, another function of old coins is to increase the power of other feng shui items. Among old coins, mainly copper coins issued by ten Emperors in Qing Dynasty (1616-1912) in China are used for feng shui items. They are as follows: Shun Ye coin, Kang Xi coin, Yong Zheng coin, Gan long coin, Jia Qing coin, Dao Guang coin, Xian feng coin, Tongzhi coin, Guang xu coin, and Suan tong coin. Among these coins, strong powers of each Emperor and absolute authority are thought to be included. In order to take in the power, they are hung in a room, buried in the ground, stuck to a feng shui ruler and placed in the front door and such. Gathering all ten coins and braiding with a red cord is named as the ten Emperors' coins. Due to the power and authority of ten Emperors, it is believed that it does not allow evil spirits to approach. However, they have very high value of antiques nowadays, and it has become difficult to obtain the real coins. So, most of the time, they are substituted with replicas.

There is an item called the "Six Emperors' old coins." Among ten Emperors mentioned above, Shun Ye coin, Kang Xi coin, Yong Zheng coin, Gan long coin, Jia Qing coin and Dao Guang coin are put together. Since they were extraordinarily powerful Emperors, their powers were supposed to be equal to the power of ten Emperors. When the six coins are hung in the house, your home will become and peaceful as well as youth and health are maintained. Furthermore, family members will be very healthy, and business and school work will proceed smoothly.

In addition, there is an item called the "Five Emperors' old coins." This is formulated by removing Emperor Dooko's old coins from "Six Emperors' old coins" and using when you hope to acquire both "power to acquire wealth" and "power of coercion" A reason to remove Dao Guang coin is that Emperor Dao Guang had authority, but he did not have the power to acquire wealth. When you want wealth, make sure you remove Dao Guang from others.

Qing coins, old coins from the Qing Dynasty, were made into the shape of a "copper money sward", and they are feng shui items to increase business and wealth fortune. This will not allow anyone who wants to take the wealth you have earned away from you, and if anyone tries to steal your money, the coins will save your money by slashing at the intruder. At the same time it has the power to slash off negative energy, and all the intrusion of demons will be eliminated if you hang it up on the front door. However, depending upon where you hang it up, the result is different. If it is to prevent theft and improve wealth, hang it near the safe or the register. If the intrusion of evil energy is to be prevented, it should be hang outside of the front door, and if the evil spirit which has intruded already needs to be eliminated, hang it where you can see in the front section as you get in from the front door.

Even if you do not have a set of all coins, just one Emperor's coin will work for you. When you are using a coin, it has to be buried on the wall or the floor of the front door.

If you insert it in the wallet, it will invite wealth as it will take a role of calling for wealth.

Improving Your Luck! Increase your power.
Charm against evil spirits
Bagua Drawn on a Copper Coin

This is a copper coin imitating ancient coins in which Bagua against evil spirits were drawn. There are two methods to utilize it: one is for self defense and another is for improving the power of other fung shui items. You walk around with it while using it as a key holder or ke eping it in the wallet at all times. It will keep you away from every misfortune.

It works as protection against traffic accidents, so keep one in your car without fail. It also works as protection against antitheft in shops. If you want to use it for the sake of increasing power, you put it under other fung shui items. Furthermore, as it has an additional Bagua power to keep your dislikes away from you, it increases fung shui power.

Buga ancient coins have two sizes: diameter 35mm and 5 yen coin size.

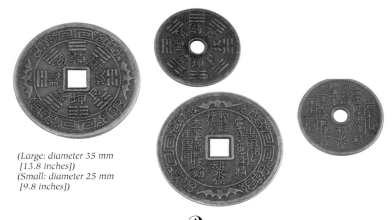

(Large: diameter 35 mm
[13.8 inches])
(Small: diameter 25 mm
[9.8 inches])

Improving your fortune!
Copper Coin Inviting Wealth

This is a copper coin imitating ancient coins in which the four Chinese characters of " inviting wealth" and "becoming richer" are engraved in the coin surface and the pictures of a dragon and Chinese phoenix in the back of the coin. The main purpose of this item is to further increase the fung shui effect of other fung shui items.

It also has the power to increase your wealth; if you wear it as a pendant or a key holder, more money will come into you. There are two sizes: diameter 45mm and 5 yen coin size. It will increase wealth if a larger coin is kept in a register and/or a safe in a store, and if a smaller one is kept in a wallet. They will invite fortune and your wealth will increase.

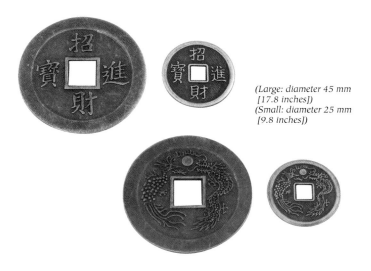

(Large: diameter 45 mm [17.8 inches])
(Small: diameter 25 mm [9.8 inches])

Increase the power of feng shui items!
Ten Powerful Emperors' Old Coins in Qing Period

Ten coins each of which was issued by ten famous Emperors in Qing period are collected. They prevent evil spirits coming near the person who possesses the coins due to the power and dignity of the Emperors. The coins will draw evil away, increase wealth and fortune and such. When they are attached to other feng shui items, they will double their strength.

Purify negative energy with sounds
Hanging Bell Type Feng Shui Wind Chime with Ten Emperors' Old Coins

This is a suitable feng shui item where a lot of water is used. When it is attached to a kitchen, kitchen doors, a bathroom or a toilet's door, ten Emperors' power and the sound of wind chime will change negative energy to positive energy. It may be a good idea to place it to prevent the intrusion of evil spirit and invite good fortune.

(Length: approximately 44 cm [17 inches])

Cut the evil spirit with the sword

Feng Shui Sword Made of Old Coins

Old coins in Qing period were made into a shape of feng shui sword. The sword will cut evil energy, and it will prevent all evil spirits intruding. You will acquire more wealth through working hard, and it will protect your wealth. If you wish to prevent burglars and hope to increase wealth, apply near a safe or a register. If you want to prevent the intrusion of evil spirits, put it near the front door.

The small size comes with a red tassel.

(Large: approximately 40 cm [15.7 inches])
(Medium: approximately 25 cm [9.9 inches])
(Small: approximately 15 cm [6 inches])

Overpowering and invites wealth
True Five Emperors' Coins

These items are hard to come by coins because they were actually in circulation. This is a collection of Shun Ye, Kang Xi, Yong Zheng, Gan long, Jia Qing coins, and it has immense power. It is very effective to overpower and invites wealth. It is valuable as an antique and is a very valuable feng shui item.

(Diameter: 2~2.5 cm [0.8 ~ 1 inch])

Brings peace and growth
Six Emperors' Old Coins

Dao Guang coin were added to five Emperors' coins and it is effective for repelling evil due to the coin's power and authority. When they are hung everywhere in the house, it brings peace and growth.

They are used with Xing water (p. 115) and shows traditional power. As they also improve the power of other feng shui items if used together with them, why don't you use them with other feng shui items? When it is applied to a Chinese unicorn (p. 68) and a wind chime, they further purify evil spirit.

Ultimate feng shui item
Five Emperors' Coin Measurement Tape

On top of a feng shui ruler (p. 21) and feng shui measurement ruler (p. 21), true five Emperors' coins are pasted in order of Shun Ye, Kang Xi, Yong Zheng, Gan long, Jia Qing coins. Primarily, they are buried directly under the ground where the front door is. It saves the intrusion of evil spirit, and the feng shui safe building is completed. If the construction of building is already completed and is difficult to bury it, place it on the doorway of the front door. There is no problem to put a door mat on top of it. This is the ultimate feng shui item to change all the bad measurements into good measurements.

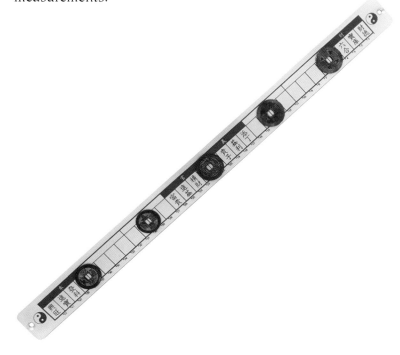

Increase the power of fung sui items!
Ten Treasure Sets

Feng shui often uses a method to increase effectiveness. "Ten treasures" is a typical item for this purpose. "Ten treasures" are as follows:

1. Gold, silver, cooper, raw iron, pearl, agate, jade, old coins which will bring wealth, and the five viscera (liver, lungs, heart, kidney and spleen) for the sake of yin and yang and the five elements.
2. Five colored threads which will bring health.
3. Typical five grains including rice, green beans, red bean, black beans and yellow beans which symbolize that there will be always food.

Besides wealth, "Ten treasures" add health, growth, prosperity and such will add to other feng shui items. Place them next to many items such as Pixiu (p. 70), an incense burner etc.

Improve your wealth!
Gold Ingot

If a gold ingot is placed close to or insert in those feng shui items particularly aimed for increasing wealth, it will increase the power of wealth. Use it with Pixiu (p. 70) and Long Gui (p. 73) or place it in a register or safe. They will become strong allies in the quest for wealth.

We often eat dumplings (gyoza), and their shape is said to originate from a gold ingot. In other words, dumplings are very auspicious food as if we are eating gold ingots. Besides made of cooper and brass, there are those made of such power stones as crystal, rutile and such.

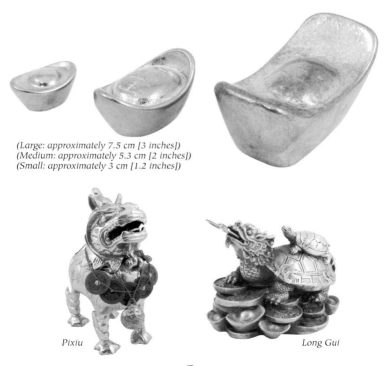

(Large: approximately 7.5 cm [3 inches])
(Medium: approximately 5.3 cm [2 inches])
(Small: approximately 3 cm [1.2 inches])

Pixiu

Long Gui

CHAPTER 8

☯

Improve your fortune using color, sound, light and fragrance!

COLOR, SOUND, LIGHT AND FRAGRANCE
HAVE ORIGINAL ENERGY. IN THIS CHAP-
TER, HOW TO DRAW OUT THE ESSEN-
TIAL POWER OF COLOR, SOUND, LIGHT
AND FRAGRANCE WILL BE INTRODUCED.

Collaboration of direction and color
Red Tassel and Yellow Tassel

A direction and its compatible color bring in good luck, and you already know about its method. There is an easy method to improve your fortune using the color effect in feng shui items. A crimson or red color is compatible with the directions of east, south east, and south. When a red tassel is hung in these directions, the energy in that room becomes very active; because of that your body and heart become healthy. Yellow is compatible with the directions of west and northwest. When a yellow tassel is hung in these directions, it becomes difficult for wealth to leave, and your fortune will improve.

(The length of each color: 60 cm [23.6 inches])

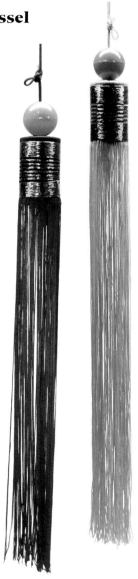

Good for Kitchen and Bathroom
Bag Specifically to Hang Crystal Ball
(Three Kinds: Red, Yellow and Purple)

A crystal ball is round and heavy, and it is best to leave it on a stand. However, if there is no place to put it, insert it in a bag specifically made for it, and hang it from the wall.

- ◆ **Red bag:** Effective to make space healthier
- ◆ **Yellow bag:** Effective to bring wealth and power
- ◆ **Purple bag:** Effective to purify energy and heal mind

Insert a crystal ball in a bag colored to meet your objectives. If a rose quartz ball is inserted in a bag, it will improve human relationships and troubles between a man and a woman. In order to improve a relationship between a husband and a wife, keep it in the bedroom. If you want to improve the relationships with the opposite sex, hang near the room. Negative energy tends to build up in the bathroom (toilet) without a window. Hang a translucent crystal ball in a purple bag and hang in the bathroom (toilet) wall. It will absorb bad energy.

(Length: approximately 40 cm [15.7 inches])

Eliminating evil born in the earth
Wind Chime
(Six Column Six Emperors' Old Coin Wind Chime)

Sound plays an important role in feng shui. In order to eliminate evil or negative energy, sound is very effective. Different kinds of sounds make different kinds of effects, and the wind chime is the best feng shui item to kill off evil born in the earth.

According to the five elements of traditional Chinese philosophy, gold is born from the earth. Bad energy born from the earth is eliminated by gold and further eliminated by sound. Hang it in the door of the kitchen, front and back door of each room, and the door to the bathroom. As you go in and out, you would hear the sound of chime, and it eliminates bad energy. When you hang it on the window about which you feel uneasy, it would remove various kinds of negative energy.

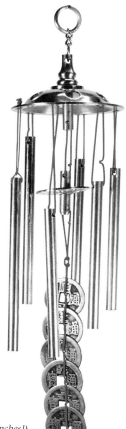

(Length: approximately 70 cm [26.6 inches])

Purify the energy floating in space
Gong

Generally we use a gong if we purify with sound. The resounding sound into far has a big role of purifying the floating energy in space. When a ship leaves a harbor, a gong is rung; it meant to remove evil energy. At one time, it was used as a sign of the enemy coming; the purpose was to rally troops.

There are two kinds of shapes of gongs: one with the protruding middle and the flat middle. There are the following characteristics: the clear sound echoes if the protruding middle gong is rung, and the sound with full impact where tempestuous sounds are intertwined with echoes if the flat middle gong is rung. It is suggested to hit the gong at the place where you want to keep off negative energy, or when you want to muster courage.

Purify negative energy with the sound of an explosion
Decorating Firecrackers

The sound of firecrackers has a strong effect to chase away negative energy. In order for negative energy not to come closer, firecracker decorations are prepared during the first day of Chinese New Year, at a wedding, and other auspicious places when happy events take place. Originally, firecrackers were not used, but fire was lit in bamboos. Each bamboo joint was destroyed after lighting the fire, and people are delighted because of the coming of spring. A bamboo symbolizes wealth, and it is said to summon prosperity and auspiciousness.

Diffuse positive energy
Crystal Multifaceted Ball

An item such as a crystal ball diffuses light, and it has an ability to diffuse energy throughout the room. A crystal multifaceted ball has various uses; it is an indispensable item for a house from which you can view the window on the balcony. The plan of the house allows wealth to run away. When there is a window in the front door or opposite of the front door, evil energy runs through the space. If so, hanging this crystal ball on the window or simply putting it will ease the strength of evil spirit. When the crystal ball is placed in a dark room, positive energy is diffused to each corner of the room, and it restrains negative energy.

Good results do not end there. The effect of positive energy revitalizes the ability to foresight and insight. It also grows and takes business into a better direction.

Furthermore, a crystal ball is effective for purifying negative energy due to a stench. The odor caused by a toilet or garbage strongly reacts against good energy negatively; therefore, it brings bad luck in feng shui. It is important to hang it in the kitchen or the bathroom (toilet) and arranges feng shui. Hang a "crystal ball inserted in a purple bag" in the bathroom (toilet) where bad energy seems to appear. It is necessary to purify thoroughly by displaying lucky bamboo, place crystal power under the sink and so on.

(Large: 16 multifaceted diameters – approximately 4 cm [1.6 inches])
(Small: 32 multifaceted diameters – approximately 3 cm [1.2 inches])

CHAPTER 9

☯

Recommended items to meet your desire and objectives

COLLECTION OF ITEMS THAT WILL WORK DEPENDING ON YOUR DESIRE AND OB-JECTIVES SPECIALLY RECOMMENDED FENG SHUI ITEMS WILL BE SELECTED.

Wealth fortune

God of Business
Copper Idol of Guan Yu of Romance of Three Kingdoms

Guan Yu (關羽雲長) who appears in Romance of Three Kingdoms with Liu Bei (劉備玄德), Zhang Fei (張飛翼德), and Zhuge Kong Ming (諸葛孔明) was an extraordinary military commander. He is very popular in China as a righteous military commander. He is also called "an elederly man" and is revered as a god.

People respect Guan Yu as the god of business. He has been deified in a bright mausoleum Kanteibyou (關帝廟) in Chinatown, Yokohama. In fact it has been said that he had invented the abacus, and his has been worshiped as a "god of wealth" by overseas Chinese known for their talents of conducting good business. He is an indispensable god for business.

Guan Yu, a god of business, will increase business and wealth. By displaying the god, you will be prosperous. It will kill off evil spirits with the sword of a military commander and bury it. If you place Long Gui (p. 73) near Guan Yu, your wealth fortune will immensely increase, and your business will prosper.

You shouldn't forget to spread copper coin replicas under Guan Yu (p. 136).

■ *All purpose feng shui item*
Flat Calming Mirror

This mirror has all-around feng shui items that improve fortune; there are a mountain filled with the energy of dragons, the lively sea, eight trigrams yin and yang and an amulet where gods' spirits reside, the sun and the moon (cosmic dual forces), light, keeping an orderly house, inviting wealth and luck, a tall headed god of happiness and so forth. Some examples of the effects of the mirror are as follows: 1) arrange feng shui, 2) invite wealth, 3) keep good networking going, 4) harmonize Shinto and Buddhism, 5) make happy life, 6) purify evil spirits, 7) suppress evil spirits, 8) balance cosmic dual forces. Its benefit is limitless.

Simply the act of placing the mirror in the front door, the living room, the store, and the office improves fortune. As it is compatible with the direction of north-east, which shows the mountains, it is recommended to put the mirror on the north eastern wall. As it is effective as a plain mirror shown in the page 54, there are many cases to substitute this as a plain mirror.

(Width: 22 cm [8.6 inches])

For prosperity
An Old Fashioned Small Abacus

This is an effective feng shui item to change bad to good energy when there is a tall building, a telegraph pole, a traffic sign near the front door or an exit, and you feel negative energy. Under these circumstances, move the beads on the numbers 3, 8, 3, 8, 3, 8, 3, 8 on this copper abacus, stabilize the numbers with an adhesive, and hang at the front door and the exit. A number 38 in the 64 hexagrams of the Book of Changes belongs to wood in the five elements of traditional Chinese philosophy, so it improve the effectiveness of "wood" and protects a misfortune of "earth." Thus, it will solve evil energy, ward off the evil energy of earth, and call good fortune in.

It is also effective to change evil to good fortune if there is a dead end, or a narrow corridor is continuing in front of the front door or the exit.

It is a useful feng shui item to place it together with the business god, Guan Yu, and promote the growth of business.

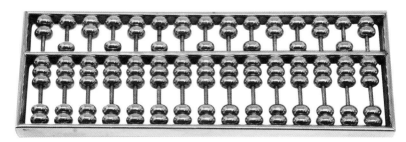

(Length: approximately 13 cm [5 inches])

Inventing wealth fortune

Bronze or Copper Medal Inviting Wealth

In order to gain the fortune of wealth, this bronze or copper medal is displayed in places such as a house, a store, an office. The four Chinese characters of inviting wealth and become richer are engraved in the medal. It is obvious to place it where money is involved. The common places to put them are a company president's room, an accounting department, near a safety vault and a cash register, and a living room.

(Diameter: approximately 20 cm [7.8 inches])

Protects evil spirits from all the directions
Bronze or Copper Medal Showing the 12 Signs of the Chinese Zodiac

Troubles which are likely to occur in all places including a house, a store, an office etc. may become calm. You can protect yourself from unforeseen troubles. Ba Gua and the 12 signs of the Chinese zodiac are engraved on the coin. Ba Gua has an effect to repel against all the disagreeable things. The 12 signs of the Chinese zodiac show that one medal covers all the directions as well as all times. It does not matter where it is placed.

Improves study and business efficiently
Nine-story Tower for Literary and Creative People

This is a feng shui item to improve your ability to concentrate when you place it on your desk. At the same time, your expressiveness becomes more active, and it improves the efficacy of work. As a result, it is said that you will have success in your life.

The tower strongly assists those whose work requires sharp brains including planning, creative and research work. Therefore, it is a recommended feng shui item for

company presidents and those who want to be entrepreneurs and creative people such as technology developers, writers and artists. In addition, it is an indispensable feng shui item for students, who need to take examinations in the near future,

Cleanse all evil spirits
Meteorite

When passing through the atmosphere, meteorites burn up all the impure materials. Looking at it from the scientific point of view, meteorites are the purest material on the earth. Having changed to power stone, it has traveled for thousands and millions of light years from a faraway place, and destiny has brought you and the meteorite together. Because the power stone had started its trip many years before you were born, there is no other item which has more energy. You have been worn out by evil spirits in the world, but by putting your heart into the power stone, you will be recharged by fresh and pure energy sent by the power stone.

It has been well known in feng shui that meteorites have the power to cleanse all evil and negative spirits. It has been said from ancient times that if you build a house where a meteorite had fell, you feel good, and if you start business, it grows without your knowledge. It is very difficult to own such a meteorite on your own, but even if you touch it in the store front where they are shown, all the evils that you have stored will be cleansed. Please try it.

It is not only you that needs the power of meteorites. The stones used for your jewelry must protect you from many troubles while you are wearing them. Please have your jewelry stones touch meteorites so that they will be able to protect you even more.

The greatest of all feng shui items! "Fate Seal"
Power Stone Seal

What is introduced here is not an ordinary fortune to make your life better. It is the ultimate feng shui item to change your energy for the better. In other words, if you have a strong will and determination to change your energy, this seal is meant for you.

There are many kinds of seals including those made of wood or animal bones or fangs. However, history goes only for a few hundred years for wood seals, and even shorter for bone and fang seals. Besides, animals were slaughtered for these purposes, so they have negative energy.

The oldest and purest materials on the earth are minerals which are buried in the ground. Those which are beautiful and precious with positive undulation are power stones; the power stone effect to change from negative to positive energy is known and proven throughout the world.

The power stone is very strong as it has absorbed the energy from ground in the earth for millions of years. It is believed that if you engrave your name onto the power stone, use it, carry it, or put it near you. The energy of power stone will become yours, and fabulous result of improving the fate will be yours. A proverb says: your name is you. This means that the name of a person or a thing expresses the substance of the person or the thing. Your name has powerful energy. The power stone with your name engraved will represent you and will become your amulet.

The natural power stone feels cooler than those made of wood or animal bones or fangs and tusks. Therefore, when you use a power stone seal, you feel its coolness as soon as you hold the seal. You then obtain the effect of high tension which makes you feel serene.

The moment you have your power stone seal in your hand and gaze at the face of the seal is the time that your energy and the power stone seal collide with each other, the synergistic effect is born, and your fortune will be lead into better. There is not anything else to produce such effect other than a power stone seal.

*To find out the details, please refer to Power Stone Nobody Has Written!! Power Stone Destiny Seal .

Feng Shui fountain which improves your financial standing

Whatever the official stance about your financial standing may be, everyone in the world wishes for financial fortune. It is our basic wish to have abundant wealth in our daily life. Well then, what is the component to bring wealth to us? In feng shui, it has been said that the energy of wealth is delivered by wind and is stopped by water. In other words, the technique is that it makes the flowing energy of wealth stop for a time, and it will be drawn in to your own space. What is needed and important here is to circulate water.

The feng shui goods that are used to meet with this need is to place a dragon hole (feng shui fountain) near the front door or to the direction of wealth. Using a strong circulatory pump, the fountain raises a heavy stone ball. An artificial hall or an opening for a dragon is created, and because the fresh water is circulated near the front door, the dragon which brings wealth and happiness will fly into the hall. As a result, wealth, human relations and various other fortunes are drawn into your own space.

In original feng shui, the purpose of researching the flow of energy in the natural world was to look for an ideal location, a dragon hole, where good energy congregates, and set up a residence or a business headquarters there, and we will have smooth and trouble free life. However, as the environment we live has been over developed and nearly destroyed, it is not possible to find dragon holes or openings. Even if we find them, it is probably someone else's property. The reason is that good dragon holes or openings grow and develop without a doubt, so it is not likely for the property to go on for a sale. Having said that, in current feng shui, we do not look for dragon holes; instead, we have researched techniques how to make dragon holes. As a result, we have come up with a dragon hole (feng shui fountain). There are smaller size fountains which can be easily placed in the house, office, front door to the store. They are popular as the art work as well. As the effect of fountains is widely known, there are many business concerns which circulate a big stone, 1 meter in diameter and 2 tons in weight, in their front doors.

It is well known that a circulating stone is made of natural crystal. Nevertheless, most crystals sold on the market are made of glass or are artificial crystals, so potential buyers must be careful. Incidentally, most of items declared as "real crystal" are actually "artificial crystal." If you want to know in detail, please refer to page 94 in my book, The Secret of Crystal.

Various types of Basins with Dragon Holes which Invite Wealth

A. Dragon king

The dragon which ranks as the king among all dragons is holding a dragon ball made of crystal, and the multiple effects are created by the crystal power and energy of the dragon. It changes the area influenced by these effects into

(Height: approximately 30 cm [11.9 inches])

powerful fung shui spot. As it is made of an alloy including copper, heat conductivity is very high. The design of the product has focused on having the most effect of eliminating negative energy.

B. A God with a Potbelly Who is One of the Seven Gods of Good Luck.

He is known as "Hotei" in Japan. As his face is beaming with smiles, it shows the best feature in physiognomy. In addition, with his potbelly, it is indisputable that money fortune comes with him. His energy along with crystal power will certainly improve your fortune.

(Height: approximately 36 cm [14 inches])

C. Affectionate Type Basin

As if it gently holds energy flown from the front, the back and above with both hands, it carefully connects with crystal power. By doing so, it creates favorable circulation for the people who gather there. Energy full of tranquility and a co-operative effect will bring fortune and luck.

(Height: approximately 16.5 cm [6.5 inches])

D. Platform Type Basin

Having invited energy from the heavens and merged with crystal power, it diffuses energy in a room. It gives courage, vitality, and liveliness to the people who gather there, and it promotes and brings better fortune and luck.

(Height: approximately 17 cm [6.7 inches])

Energy is flowing with wind and scattering about,
and it is stopped by water

International Fengshui Association

Until 10 years ago or so, not many people have heard of "feng shui." However, it has become a huge boom in recent years in the world. I don't believe it is simply a fad; I feel it has taken root.

Feng shui draws a line from fortune telling. It is learning which has progressed in the long history of China and continues on; it is the study of environmental maintenance, data, and statistics. It is common knowledge that the study of fortune telling based on Chinese twelve year cycle and the study of directions practiced in Japan have originated in feng shui. Feng shui is a science of problem solving for which people have. However, there is a fear of feng shui improperly used. There may be those who have not sufficiently acquired the knowledge of feng shui practicing it, the standard of feng shui practitioners may vary enormously, or some might even practice with wrong knowledge.

International Fengshui Association is actively involved to spread honest and legitimate feng shui.

Activities:

- A certification examination and giving lectures
- Improving the feng shui of houses, stores, companies, establishments etc.
- Advertising and publishing legitimate feng shui
- Hold and promote events pertaining to feng shui
- Gather and supply feng shui information
- Authorize feng shui speciality shop and spread legitimate feng shui items

The list of authorized shops

Feng Shui Kaiun Chushin (Asakusa) and Feng Shui Kaiun Chushin (Odaiba) are specialty shops which were authorized by International Fengshui Association. There is a world of difference in terms of power within the same form of feng shui items. It is important that you would choose legitimate feng shui items that were manufactured using traditional materials and methods.

The Office of International Fengshui Association
〒111-0032 1-16-9 Asakusa, Taito-ku, Tokyo, Japan
Tel: 03-3845-6808   Fax: 03-3845-8236
www.fu-sui.com

Biographic Note

Masahiro Tsukada, the author, is a leading expert of International Feng Shui, Directions to Harmony: *How to Use Feng Shui in Your Daily Life (An Illustrated Guide to Tranquility and Good Fortune)*. Traditional feng shui items which has been used to improve fortune were defined in this book, and it was translated into Chinese in China, the home of feng shui. It has become an important feng shui textbook. His name in Chinese is Andy Wong (黄 安迪). The author has a thorough knowledge of mineralogy where power stone had originated, and he has published a number of books about minerals, power stone, crystal, and so on. In addition, he is the chief director of International Fengshui Association and the chief director of International Power Stones Association.

Contact address pertaining to this information

Feng Shui Kaiun Chushin (Asakusa)
〒111-0032
1-39-11 Asakusa, Taito-ku, Tokyo, Japan
(in front of Asakusa Kokaido 浅草公会堂前)
Tel: 03-3843-2468
Fax: 03-3843-8236
www.chugokuya.com

Feng Shui Kaiun Chushin (Odaiba)
〒135-0091
1-6-1 Daiba, Minato-ku, Tokyo, Japan
Odaiba DECKS Tokyo Beach Bldg.
Tel & Fax: 03-3599-6868

Feng Shui Kaiun Chushin New York (風水改運中心NY)
595 River Rd., Edgewater, NJ 07020 USA
(Mitsuwa Market Place内)
Tel: 917-653-4716
E-mail: fengshui@cybercap.com   www.fengshuikaiun.com

Publication data:
Author: Masahiro Tsukada
Published by AK Family Corporation (Sean Shono, Chief Director of NY Branch, IFA)
Producer: Motohisa Tsukada
Director: Harehisa Tsukada
Photo: Kazuo Kadota

Editor & Coordinator: Mikiko Nakayama
Designer: Harumi Okamatsu
Translated by: Yasuyo Aso Battenfeld

Printed in China